Petra Hüttemann

Benefits of a law firm's website

FRANKFURTER SCHRIFTEN ZUM MARKETING FÜR FINANZDIENSTLEISTUNGEN

Herausgegeben von Prof. Dr. Ralf Jasny

ISSN 1861-0978

1 *Christof Jauernig*
Führungssysteme im Franchising von Banken
Anforderungen, Auswahl und Umsetzung im Privatkundengeschäft
ISBN 3-89821-528-8

2 *Christine Schlitz*
Anlageberatungshonorare im Private Banking
ISBN 3-89821-540-7

3 *Petra Hüttemann*
Benefits of a law firm's website
ISBN 978-389821-554-1

Petra Hüttemann

BENEFITS OF A LAW FIRM'S WEBSITE

ibidem-Verlag
Stuttgart

Bibliografische Information der Deutschen Nationalbibliothek
Die Deutsche Nationalbibliothek verzeichnet diese Publikation in der Deutschen Nationalbibliografie; detaillierte bibliografische Daten sind im Internet über http://dnb.d-nb.de abrufbar.

Bibliographic information published by the Deutsche Nationalbibliothek
Die Deutsche Nationalbibliothek lists this publication in the Deutsche Nationalbibliografie; detailed bibliographic data are available in the Internet at http://dnb.d-nb.de.

A CIP catalogue record for this book is available from:
Die Deutsche Bibliothek
http://dnb.ddb.de

Publisher's note: This book has been produced from ready-to-print data provided by the author(s) and/or inidividual contributors. The publisher makes no representation, express or implied, with regard to the accuracy of the information contained in this book and cannot accept any legal responsibility or liability for any errors or omissions that may have been made.

∞

Gedruckt auf alterungsbeständigem, säurefreien Papier
Printed on acid-free paper

ISSN: 1861-0978

ISBN-10: 3-89821-554-7
ISBN-13: 978-3-89821-554-1

All rights reserved. No part of this publication may be reproduced, stored in or introduced into a retrieval system, or transmitted, in any form, or by any means (electronical, mechanical, photocopying, recording or otherwise) without the prior written permission of the publisher. Any person who does any unauthorized act in relation to this publication may be liable to criminal prosecution and civil claims for damages.

Printed in Germany

Content

Tables and figures

Abbreviations

B-2-B	Business-to-Business
BRAO	Federal Regulations for Attorneys (Bundesrechtsanwaltsordnung)
eCRM	electronic customer relationship management
et seq.	and the following (one page)
et sqq.	and the following (several pages)
etc.	et cetera
e.g.	for example (exempli gratia)

1 Introduction

1.1 Problem definition

The Internet is playing an increasing role in our everyday private and business lives.[1] New opportunities are arising all the time and many organisations have already set up websites allocating substantial budgets each year to keep them up and running.

This observation also holds true for the legal sector. All international law firms and many national and regional ones have their own websites. The legal sector has only had fairly limited marketing opportunities this far but this is starting to change and new interesting opportunities are beginning to open up.[2]

Many law firms are not taking full advantage of modern innovations in website design, content, and structure and their websites often prove to be of little use to their clients. One possible reason for this is that law firms are failing to take their clients' needs and expectations into account.

Realising client expectations may aid a law firm to better align its online strategies, generate more benefit for its clients, and differentiate itself from its competitors.

1.2 Objectives

The main focus of this thesis is to identify the benefits that law firms and their clients can derive from a law firm website.

Given that law firms generally have to benefit their clients before they can benefit themselves the second focus of this thesis is to explore

[1] See SCHNELLER (2004) page 1-35

[2] See 2.3 for more information on marketing restrictions in the legal sector

the clients' needs, expectations and benefits; and their potential impact on the client / law firm relationship.

The research results form the basis for recommending possible ways and strategies for improving the websites of law firms.

1.3 Approach

In order to achieve these objectives, the following steps are carried out during the study and the thesis is structured as follows:

1) Analyse the business particularities for law firms in Germany: In order to assess the possibilities for improvement open to law firms in the German legal market it is important to analyse the current market situation and evaluate the marketing restrictions imposed on law firms by legislation and the nature of the services they provide.
2) Literature research on online strategies and success drivers of corporate websites: Studies on corporate websites will be used as a starting point for a more in-depth analysis of websites in the legal sector. This will include the identification of possible online strategies, potential user groups and the success factors applicable to websites.
3) Assumptions on benefits of law firms' websites: A benefits model for the possible benefits that a law firm's website can offer to clients and firms is developed based on previous studies.
4) Building of hypotheses: The hypotheses are built based on the model of possible client benefits.
5) Applicability testing: The hypotheses are validated through empirical research.

6) Recommendations for an online strategy for law firms: Recommendations for an online strategy for law firms are made based on the results of the interviews.

2 The legal sector

This chapter analyses the environment of law firms in the German legal market with the focus on selling and marketing legal services.

2.1 The German legal market

In the last few years the legal market has come under pressure due to economic weakness in most western countries. This caused an increase in competition as the number of deals and their volume dropped. The increased competition forced many law firms to rethink their strategy and structure and several law firms merged in order to stay competitive in the changed market place. Although some law firms still have a descending or stagnating development in turnover, some of the merged firms managed to increase their turnover by as much as nearly 50%[3] in 2003 (compared to 2002).[4]

Figure 1: The 10 highest grossing law firms in 2003 globally[5]

Rank	Firm	Revenue	Lawyers	Equity Partners	Global Presence	
2004		Gross	Firm total	Firm total	Countries in which firm has offices	Lawyers outside home country
1	Clifford Chance	$ 1,552,500,000	2,684	406	20	62%
2	Skadden, Arps. Slate, Meagher & Flom	$ 1,330,000,000	1,650	350	12	10%

[3] Increase of turnover was achieved through mergers and acquisitions not through natural growth.
[4] See GRIFFITHS, A. (2004) page 11 et sqq.
[5] The chart is based on 'The global 100' list compiled by AUTHOR UNKNOWN (2004d).

Rank	Firm	Revenue	Lawyers	Equity Partners	Global Presence	
2004		Gross	Firm total	Firm total	Countries in which firm has offices	Lawyers outside home country
3	Freshfields Bruckhaus Deringer	$ 1,283,000,000	2,225	516	19	66%
4	Linklaters	$ 1,176,500,000	2,000	390	23	55%
5	Baker & McKenzie	$ 1,134,000,000	3,035	611	38	83%
6	Allen & Overy	$ 1,065,500,000	1,879	312	20	53%
7	Jones Day	$ 1,035,000,000	1,970	427	12	24%
8	Latham & Watkins	$ 1,033,000,000	1,513	367	10	19%
9	Sidley Austin Brown & Wood	$ 926,000,000	1,421	288	7	11%
10	Mayer, Brown, Rowe & Maw	$ 813,000,000	1,249	426	5	27%

The list of 'The global 100'[6] is compiled each year which allows the reader to view a firm's performance over time and to compare the performance of firms. It has to be mentioned though that revenues and numbers of lawyers and partners are not suitable to assess a law firm's economic performance in detail, but this list gives a first impression of the legal market at present. Figure 1 gives an overview over the 10 highest grossing law firms in the world. It shows that the firm with the most equity partners and lawyers, or the one that operates in the most

[6] Author unknown (2004d)

countries does not necessarily have to be the one that achieves the highest revenues.[7]

The fact that big American law firms are pushing into the legal markets in Europe and especially into the German market increases the competition in Europe. The American law firms managed to increase their turnover in Europe in 2003 and although the English Partnerships manage to win more mandates, the American Partnerships manage quite often to win those mandates that offer more profit. In the ranking of 'The lawyer Euro 100'[8] it is remarkable that nine US-partnerships can be found within the Top 50.[9]

In the years after the 'IT-bubble' burst in 2001 several law firms in Germany encountered severe problems due to the overall economic downturn, mismanagement and inefficient structures (e.g. PWC Veltins).[10] These problems led to loss of partners and in some cases even to the closing of entire offices (e.g. Ey Law Luther Menold lost partners in Hamburg and the entire office in Bochum left the partnership in summer 2003).[11]

In 2003 fewer big deals took place than in 2002. The trend of the years before was continued. There were only few exceptionally big deals, but overall massive losses in volume and value of the signed deals picture the general market situation for law firms in Germany.[12]

This recession affected nearly all law firms in almost all practice areas. Especially the areas Equity-Finance and M&A were affected by this, but in 2003 these practice areas recovered slightly.[13]

Most law firms try to deal with these challenges by restructuring their organisation and their client portfolio. In the past this also meant

---

[7] See GRIFFITHS, C. (2004) page 32 et sqq.
[8] See AUTHOR UNKNOWN (2004b) page 14
[9] See AUTHOR UNKNOWN (2004b) page 10 et sqq.
[10] See HÜMMER, U. and JATZKOWSKI, A. (2004) page 26
[11] See HÜMMER, U. and JATZKOWSKI, A. (2004) page 26
[12] See HÜMMER, U. and JATZKOWSKI, A. (2004) page 21
[13] See AUTHOR UNKNOWN (2004c) page 18

consolidation[14] and although the top law firms managed to increase turnover in the year 2003 it is very likely that this trend is continued in 2004.[15]

It is important for a law firm to be visible in the market and to show its skills, experience and successes. Many law firms have recognised this need already as can be seen from the fact that *"since 1989, marketing costs have grown faster than all other operating expenses at large firms."*[16]

Apart from restructuring and monitoring costs it will be essential for law firms to stay ahead of their competitors and to find new ways of marketing and delivering their services to their clients. General marketing activities and especially online marketing activities can help a law firm to achieve this goal.

2.2 Selling legal services

The legal sector is a service industry and therefore several things have to be kept in mind when selling and marketing legal services.[17]

Services have distinct characteristics that influence marketing decisions in service companies. Services are intangible, which means that they can – unlike goods – usually not be seen, felt, tasted, or touched. They are performed by people for people and underlie a huge variety of influencing factors, such as the mood of the customer or employee or the time of day (Heterogeneity). Most services are sold first and then produced and consumed simultaneously (e.g. a contract can only be written and sold, once the client provided all the details). The customer himself will often be a part of the production process (Simultaneous production and consumption). And services are perishable, which means they cannot be saved, stored, resold or

[14] See HÜMMER, U. and JATZKOWSKI, A. (2004) page 26
[15] See GRIFFITHS, A. (2004) page 11 et sqq.
[16] AUTHOR UNKNOWN (2004a) page 56
[17] See ZEITHAML, V. and BITNER, M. J. (2000) page 2-23

returned. Therefore the demand of services has to be determined carefully over time and the capacities of the organisation have to be planned accordingly.[18]

Selling a service therefore is different to selling a product in some respects. The personal component is far more important for selling a service than for selling a product, as a service is usually produced and consumed simultaneously. This leads to problems in quality assurance, as it is very hard to ensure a certain level of service quality over time. Apart from ensuring consistent quality it is just as difficult to demonstrate the quality and value of the service to customers[19]. Word-of-mouth recommendations are therefore very important in the service industry. Another obstacle to promotional campaigns is the intangibility of services, which can be overcome by introducing symbols, or logos, which help the customer relate to a certain service.[20]

The specific characteristics of services have certain effects on the selling of legal services and implications for the marketing activities of law firms. The main problem is caused by the intangibility of legal services, which conflicts with the client's desire to assess and measure the likely quality of the legal service in advance. Law firms have to be aware of this and they need to create tangible components of their service by providing their clients with physical 'evidence' of their service quality, e.g. by designing their offices and waiting areas, by demonstrating constant training, etc.[21]

The fact that legal services are perishable causes also problems for law firms, which can only partially be solved with marketing activities. Law firms have to provide their service capacities whether it is fully employed or not. This results in high overheads as rent and salaries

---

[18] See CZINKOTA, M. R. and KOTABE, M. (2001) page 260 et sqq.; MEFFERT, H. and BRUHN, M. (2003) page 64-66 and ZEITHAML, V. and BITNER, M. J. (2000) page 12 et seq.
[19] See NEAL, C., QUESTER, P. and HAWKINS, D. (2002) page 152 et sqq.
[20] See CZINKOTA, M. R. and KOTABE, M. (2001) page 396
[21] See RÖMERMANN, R. (2003) page 68 et sqq.

have to be paid anyway. Marketing can help to smoothen out times of lower workload and help the law firm to be more profitable.[22]

2.3 Restrictions to marketing in the German legal market

German unfair competition laws are very strict, especially for lawyers and law firms.[23] Although the restrictions have been loosened in the past few years they still impose a number of restrictions on marketing oriented law firms.

Generally it can be stated that advertising is only allowed for law firms if its format and content is designed in such a way as to inform clients of the work and expertise of the law firm factually. Advertising and marketing activities aiming at winning a certain mandate are not allowed, as they conflict with the unfair competition laws. But activities aiming at the acquisition of a certain client or client group are allowed as long as it can be assumed that the potential mandates are not specified in number and content.[24] This restrictions, that have been in place for decades (some even centuries), led to a rather limited use of colours in the design of office and advertising material of law firms.

A law firm's website on the Internet does not seem to be violating the unfair competition laws, as it aims at several – not to say all – existing and future clients. A law firm's website has to be designed according to current laws, just like any other corporate website. Some of the information that has to be accessible is for example name and address of the responsible, commercial register, sales tax identification number, etc. The rules that apply for any e-marketing activities such as newsletters and unsolicited emails in the B-2-B sector apply for the legal service sector as well.

---

[22] See RÖMERMANN, R. (2003) page 72 et sqq.
[23] See HOEFLMAYER, D. (2003) page 49
[24] See HOEFLMAYER, D. (2003) page 52 and HOSS, D. (2003) page 20 et sqq.

Disobeying the unfair competition laws and the code of professional conduct[25] can seriously harm the law firm's business and reputation. The legal actions that parties, harmed by the unfair advertising, can take are based on the unfair competition laws e.g. declarations to cease and desist or based on the BRAO[26] e.g. warnings, reprovals, or fines of up to € 25.000. It is even possible to exclude the lawyer from the Bar Association and to ban him from practising for up to five years.[27]

The prevailing case law indicates that the laws restricting marketing are becoming more liberal.[28] Considering the tense situation and the increasing competition in this market it seems obvious that this strict regimentation will be loosened further in the future.[29]

Although law firms have several restrictions imposed on them it has to be mentioned that they also have several legal possibilities for advertising and marketing in general and in an online environment. Law firms should therefore use the marketing possibilities they have and make themselves seen in the marketplace.[30]

---

[25] Standesrechtliche Bestimmungen für den Anwaltsberuf
[26] Federal Regulations for Attorneys
[27] See HOEFLMAYER, D. (2003) page 52 et seq.
[28] See HOEFLMAYER, D. (2003) page 53
[29] See HOEFLMAYER, D. (2003) page 53 and STEINBEIS, M. (2004)
[30] See HOSS, D. (2003) page 20 et sqq.

3 Corporate websites

This chapter gives an overview over online strategies and success drivers of websites as identified in literature. The definitions of the terms 'e-business' and 'e-commerce' vary in literature, here they are used interchangeably and they describe the production, trade and delivery process of products and services with the use of modern information and communication technology. The findings of the studies concerning online strategies and success drivers of websites are used as a starting point for the exploration of the possible benefits that can derive from a law firm's website.

3.1 Common online strategies

Before examining online strategies in the legal market this chapter gives an overview of how online strategies are included in the overall corporate and business strategy.

3.1.1 Online strategies in the wider business context

An online strategy has to be examined in the context of the corporate and business strategy of the organisation. It is part of the strategic plan of the organisation and can not be evaluated without viewing the wider business context.

The corporate strategy gives a rather broad guideline for the organisation and determines what business the organisation is operating in (e.g. the legal sector). The business strategy describes more detailed the market the firm is operating in and what position the firm is aiming at (e.g. market leader for M&A).[31] The online strategy defines how the available technology should be used.

[31] See MAISTER, D. (1993) page 223 et sqq. and MEFFERT, H. and BRUHN, M. (2003) page 157

Figure 2: Online strategy in the context of corporate and business strategy[32]

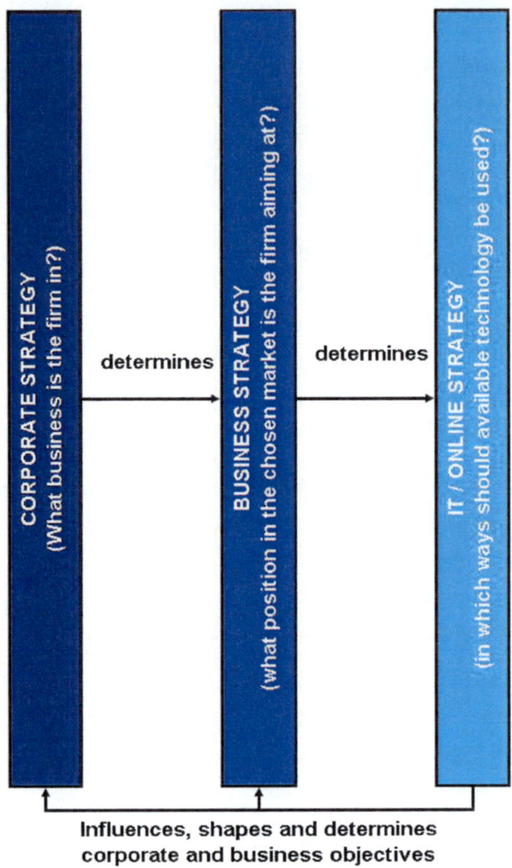

The relationship between the online strategy and the corporate and business strategy is bi-directional. The corporate and the business strategy determine in some ways the online strategy, as it describes how the available technology should be used to best support the corporate

[32] Own illustration, based on SUSSKIND, R. (1998) page 226 et seq.

and business objectives. But the online strategy also influences, shapes and determines the corporate and business strategies of the firm, as it enables change and innovation and even creates new fields of business.[33]

3.1.2 Online strategies in the legal market

Each organisation facing the decision whether and how to start its online activities, should define a clear online strategy that states the purpose of the website, the planned activities, the budget and the expected outcome of these actions. Basis of an e-business strategy is the analysis of the existing as well as the future market environment and the own core competencies and resources.[34]

According to INTENDANCE[35] the possibilities range from a mere 'brochure website' which provides basic information about the firm to a 'marketing website' which contains publications and other content of interest to the target audience. A 'personalised website' which grants every registered user password-protected access to an extranet that contains information of specific interest would be the most elaborate website type. It has to be mentioned that costs increase as the depth of the website and the integration of the customer increase.[36]

SUSSKIND differentiates between four generations of websites in the legal sector, depending on their interaction with the client. The first generation is a website which only displays brochure and marketing material. Websites of the second generation can be compared to legal libraries with a multitude of books, articles and other publications that are rather grouped by type than by content. Websites of the third generation are focused on legal disciplines and are therefore an advancement of second-generation websites. SUSSKIND calls the fourth

[33] See SUSSKIND, R. (1998) page 226 et sqq.
[34] STRAUSS, R. and SCHODER, D. (2002) page 68
[35] INTENDANCE is a London and Paris based websites development and management company
[36] AUTHOR UNKNOWN (2004e) page 17

and final generation of websites 'real life' sites and he sees them as the dominant form of websites in the future. They will offer online-guidance to users and give useful advice on a variety of legal issues.[37]

Organisations that are entering the Internet usually start with a basic website that informs about their business and gives customers and prospective customers the possibility to contact the organisation. And as they gain more experience they add other features like online-shops, newsletters or portals to their website.

Both theories give the impression that an organisations ultimate goal should be to develop a website that is on the highest possible level. But they both fail to prove whether this is what customers want and whether websites like this can deliver benefit to the customers and the organisations alike.

3.2 User groups

Each website has a multitude of visitors coming from different backgrounds and with different needs and expectations concerning the structure and content of the website. The visitors can be clustered in user groups with similar needs and expectations. A website usually attracts customers, prospective customers, employees, future employees, competitors and journalists.

3.2.1 Customers and prospective customers

Customers and prospective customers are not a homogenous group and depending on the industry the organisation operates in, they can be single customers, businesses or a mixture of both.[38]

Their needs and expectations vary depending on their personal education (e.g. lawyer or non-lawyer) and the reasons for contracting

---

[37] See SUSSKIND, R. (1998) page liv

[38] See MADEJA, N. and SCHODER, D. (2003)

the organisation (e.g. when contracting a law firm for solving an IPR dispute or for solving problems that arose after a small car accident).

Another factor that is important for describing this user group is their online behaviour. Their use of the Internet and the extend to which they use it in their business life probably depends on their general acceptance of modern communication technologies. Clients that frequently use the Internet are likely to be more frequent visitors to law firms' websites than clients that do not use the Internet.

In order to narrow the group of clients and prospective clients down, this paper concentrates on clients and prospective clients of international law firms. Therefore this group probably contains governmental institutions and big organisations that either operate internationally or do complex deals in their home country.

As an analysis of all user groups is not possible in this paper due to size restrictions, the focus will be on customers and prospective customers or clients and prospective clients in the case of a law firm. The other user groups are mentioned in the following for completeness and many of the findings on clients and prospective clients should be applicable to these groups as well.

3.2.2 Employees and future employees

A corporate website is a good possibility for an organisation to introduce itself to a wider audience than in any other media. A good corporate website with clearly stated objectives and which shows the opportunities the organisation has to offer to its employees, can not only help to attract new employees (in the case of a law firm this would be associates and partners) but it can also help the organisation to develop its corporate identity and to create a common understanding of its values and its mission and vision.

3.2.3 Competitors

Each website offers valuable information on the organisation - in this case the law firm. Customers and prospective customers do not only use this information but it is a good source of up-to-date market information for competitors. Information on locations, size, practice areas and even partners and associates of a law firm can easily be obtained on the Internet. As it is important for any organisations to stay informed on their competitors' activities it can be assumed that corporate websites are regularly monitored by other organisations operating in the same market.

3.2.4 Press

Journalists often research for their articles on the Internet and a corporate website is always a good starting point when gathering information on an organisation. It can be assumed that journalists visit a law firm’s website for general market information and information on partners and associates.

3.3 Success drivers of websites

There are various factors that influence the possible success of a corporate website and which have a different impact on the possible benefits it can deliver to its users and providers. Therefore the success drivers are examined in this chapter and they serve as a basis for the benefits model that is developed in chapter 3.4.

3.3.1 Overview

In this paper a success driver of a website is defined as a feature[39] or function[40] embedded in the website which offers benefit to the user or

[39] In this paper features are defined as properties of websites, e.g. availability.
[40] In this paper a function is defined as an element of a website which can be technical (e.g. frames, navigation etc.) or which can be related to the content of the website (e.g.

the owner of the website. Benefits that the organisation can deliver to its customers will increase satisfaction, which in turn is a good basis for the development of a profitable long-term relationship with that customer. Customer satisfaction and retention have a positive impact on the business success of the organisation and organisations should explore all possible ways of offering benefits to their customers.[41]

A vast amount of possible success drivers of websites can be identified in literature. Depending on the author's background and the focus of the research the numbers and the respective importance of success drivers vary. The features and functions that are likely to be success drivers – as identified in the literature – can be summarised in three feature categories.[42] This list does not claim to be complete, but the listed features seem to be the most important and relevant for the purpose of this paper. They are used to construct the client and firm benefits model and they are the foundation for the empirical part of this paper.

---

search function, publications databases, etc.) or which enables user-interaction (e.g. newsletters, chat rooms, etc.).

[41] See FASSNACHT, M. (1999) pages 317-321

[42] MADEJA, N. and SCHODER, D. (2003)

Figure 3: Success drivers of websites - overview

Feature category	Feature[43]	Description	Function / Example
Technical features	Accessibility[44]	Website is accessible with a variety of browsers and technical standards	Limited use of frames and animated pictures and movies
	Availability[45]	Website is available 24/7, site breakdowns are minimised	Good website management
	Security[46]	Data transfer and user data is secure and protected from third parties	SSL-encodement, firewalls,...
Content-related features	Immediacy[47]	Website is updated frequently and the content is always up-to-date	Content management
	Information Richness[48]	Website contains different types of content and content of different quality	Corporate details, publications, useful links;...

[43] The features are listed in alphabetical order.
[44] See MADEJA, N. and SCHODER, D. (2003)
[45] See AUTHOR UNKNOWN (2001) page 387
[46] See AUTHOR UNKNOWN (2001) page 372, 386 et seq.; FRITZ, W. (2004) page 268et seq. and KENYON, H. (2000) page 7 et seq.
[47] See MADEJA, N. and SCHODER, D. (2003)
[48] See MADEJA, N. and SCHODER, D. (2003)

	Media Richness[49]	Website contains different media types – this should not conflict with accessibility	Use of audio, video and image files where appropriate
Features related to user-interaction	Customisation[50]	Website can be adapted to different user preferences	Customer log-in, suggestions for further reading/shopping
	Connectivity	Website helps users to connect with other users easily	Chat rooms, discussion forums
	Ease-of-use[51]	Website can be browsed easily and content is displayed transparently	Clear navigation, search function,...
	Interactivity[52]	Website enables users to communicate bi-directional with the organisation	Contact forms, newsletters, chat rooms

[49] See MADEJA, N. and SCHODER, D. (2003)

[50] See AUTHOR UNKNOWN (2001) page 372; FRITZ, W. (2004) page 139 and MADEJA, N. and SCHODER, D. (2003)

[51] See AUTHOR UNKNOWN (2001) page 372, 386 and NIELSEN, J and NORMAN, A. (2000)

[52] See MADEJA, N. and SCHODER, D. (2003)

3.3.2 Technical features

The technical features support the other two feature categories, as there is no opportunity to create benefit or achieve success without a technically well functioning website.[53]

Technical features such as accessibility, availability and security issues are essential for the success of a website.

It is obvious that a website has to be available and accessible as it is impossible to pass on information or even conduct business over the Internet, if the corporate website is not up and functioning.

And the need for stricter security regulations is increasing as the threats to websites and its users increase. Hackers around the world are developing new methods for getting access to confidential information and threats like viruses and 'phishing attacks'[54] are constantly threatening everybody doing business on the Internet. In an article published on the PWC website[55], KENYON[56] names the main security issues that have to be dealt with. He identifies 5 major problems that have to be solved by organisations in order to ensure a secure connection with their customers over the Internet. Organisations have to verify the identity of parties in a transaction (authentication) and to ensure that information is not altered in transit (integrity). They have to prevent others from eavesdropping (privacy), ensure non-repudiation of their transactions and deal with the interoperability of their website meaning that the organisation needs to have operating rules that span geo-political boundaries.[57]

---

[53] See also Figure 5: Relationship between features and benefits

[54] 'Phishing' is a technique used to gain personal information for purposes of identity theft, using fraudulent e-mail messages that appear to come from legitimate businesses. These authentic-looking messages are designed to fool recipients into divulging personal data such as account numbers and passwords, credit card numbers and Social Security numbers. (Definition found on www.computerworld.com)

[55] www.pwc.com

[56] See KENYON, H. (2000) page 7 et seq.

[57] See KENYON, H. (2000) page 7

If a website is not accessible due to technical incompatibility, is not available due to bad website management, or if the customer feels that his data is not transferred and stored safely, the success of the website is at stake. But this does not mean, that a website which is accessible and available and that gives its users a sense of security is successful. Users assume that a website is technically functioning and they probably do not visit a dysfunctional website or visit it just once.

3.3.3 Content-related features

The content of a corporate website is the key to its success as it offers benefits to the users who visit the website. The main content-related features are Immediacy, Information Richness and Media Richness and they are described in detail in the following.

Immediacy is the most obvious feature a website should have, as out-of-date information is of no use to anybody.[58] But still many corporate websites contain out-of-date content and are not updated frequently, if at all. This means that failing to display up-to-date content reduces the benefit a website can offer to its visitors and it can even cause harm to the websites' users as the content can lead to decisions based on wrong information. And in return this can reduce the possible success of the website and of the organisation in general.

Immediacy of content alone is not sufficient as a visitor to a corporate website does not only expect the information to be up-to-date but also to be extensive enough to satisfy his needs. Therefore it is important that a corporate website is rich in information. MADEJA and SCHODER state that 'a general corporate website is found to be a success driver if it is rich in information (content) and updated frequently.'[59] PIIRTO HEATH supports this, as she states that content is the only thing that is of real importance to customers. *"Our experts*

[58] See MEFFERT, H. and BÖING, C. (2000) page 16
[59] See MADEJA, N. and SCHODER, D. (2003)

unanimously agreed that successful sites are the ones that offer content that is useful and relevant to visitors.'[60]

A decade ago nearly all published content was print-based, which meant that the reader had to access the information in a rather linear fashion, from the beginning to the finish. But nowadays it is common to offer multi-media publications and to display multi-media content on websites. This allows the user to browse through the content and to access additional information on the investigated topic; e.g. a text-description is enhanced by a short video and sound.[61] But media richness does not mean to pile up as many different media as possible but it means that different media should be used to highlight or explain different issues in an appropriate manner. The users technical standards should be considered before including big media files. A few years ago many websites contained vast amounts of different media without a clear link to the published content, but this has changed and media used on websites now tends to support the published content. PIIRTO HEATH who states, *"Now we are seeing smarter graphics that play a specific role in a site"*, supports this.[62]

3.3.4 User-interaction related features

The third feature category contains features related to user-interaction because a website only makes sense, if its content can be accessed by the users and if it allows the users to interact with the organisation and with each other. This category therefore includes the features Customisation, Connectivity, Ease-of-use and Interaction, which are explained in detail in the following.

Customisation or personalisation of websites has become more and more important in the last years as the number of available

---

[60] PIIRTO HEATH, R. (1997) page 52

[61] See SUSSKIND, R. (1998) page xvii et sqq.

[62] PIIRTO HEATH, R. (1997) page 53

websites has increased steadily[63] and the websites themselves have increased in depth and breadth due to improved server technology. This makes it harder for users to find the desired content easily and as many of them do not have unlimited time at their hands, it is interesting for them to limit the displayed information or to restrict it to content that is valuable to them. Many organisations have therefore started to offer the possibility to access personalised content after registering on the website to their customers.

A good way for organisations to help their customers find the desired information fast is to help the users to connect with each other and to exchange knowledge and discuss problems. Installing chat rooms and discussion forums on the corporate website increases the Connectivity of the website and helps the customers to network.[64]

Another important thing to keep in mind when designing a website is ease-of-use or usability.[65] Switching costs are low on the Internet[66] and no user wants to learn how a website works before he can use it. Currently there are only few websites around which make it easy for users to grasp the content of the website and its possibilities. *'Usability studies typically find a success rate of less than 50%'.*[67] As the quoted studies are several years old, it is very likely that things have changed since then, but there is probably still room for improvement when it comes to usability.

Websites often enable a two-way interaction between users and organisations and this allows for quick information exchange, e.g. via an email contact sheet or a forum where expert advice is given by qualified employees. *'For business customers is the interactivity most important for a corporate website [...].'*[68]

---

[63] See AUTHOR UNKNOWN (2001) page 366 and PIIRTO HEATH (1997) page 50
[64] See SUSSKIND, R. (1998) page xiv
[65] See NIELSEN, J. and NORMAN D. A. (2000)
[66] See AUTHOR UNKNOWN (2001) page 369
[67] NIELSEN, J. and NORMAN D. A. (2000)
[68] MADEJA, N. and SCHODER, D. (2003)

3.4 Benefits of a law firms website

The integration of a corporate website in the overall business processes can generate benefits for the organisation as well as for its customers. The benefits that come from the website have to be analysed in order to measure their importance and their overall impact on the business success of the organisation.

3.4.1 Overview

The benefits deriving from a corporate website in the legal sector have not yet been examined. As a consequence this chapter will be based on the findings on the website features and the respective functions as described in chapter 3.3. These theories are used to develop a benefits model that serves as a basis for the building of the hypotheses and for structuring the empirical part of this paper.

The number of existing website functions is too big to serve as a basis for the development of the benefits model; therefore, they are grouped in functional areas. There are probably some functions that could be grouped in more than just one functional area. Here they are grouped under the heading that they fit best. The technical features are not listed here, as the focus of this paper is on the possible benefits of the four functional areas based on content-related features and features related to user-interaction.

Figure 4 lists the functional areas according to the feature category they are based on and gives a short description of each functional area. For the corporate websites of law firms four functional areas are identified.

Figure 4: Functional areas of corporate websites - overview

Functional areas based on content-related features	**Functional areas based on features related to user-interaction**
Access to law firm: The functional area 'access to law firm' provides information on the law firm and its partners and associates in various formats e.g. online search function, descriptive texts, virtual tours, etc.	Customised Access: The functional area 'customised access' includes all functions that enable the interaction between the law firm and its clients e.g. extranets and restricted areas for clients.
Information providing: The functional area 'information providing' comprises all information that is provided free of charge to clients and prospective clients e.g. publications, event calendars, newsletter, etc.	Online Delivery: The functional area 'online delivery' describes the entire process of online service delivery and the providing of premium content e.g. templates, guidelines, legal online advice, etc.

Figure 5 describes the relationship between features, functional areas and benefits. It can be seen that the technical features merely support the content-related features and the features related to user-interaction and that they serve as a basis for a functioning website. Each functional area generates benefit for the client and the law firm, but there are also firm benefits that derive from client benefits. The client and the firm benefits coming from a law firm's website are described in the following subchapters in detail.

Figure 5: Relationship between features and benefits[69]

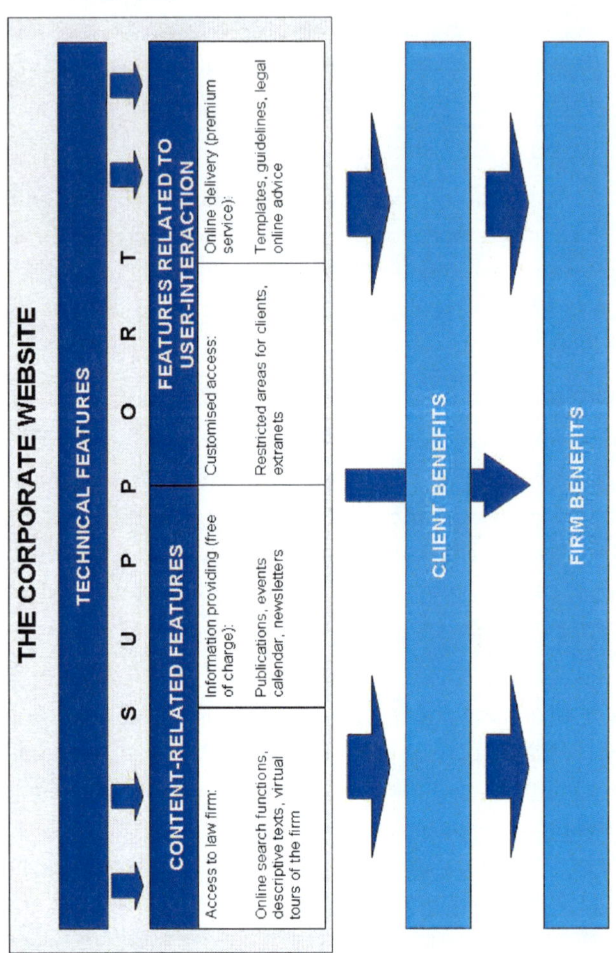

[69] own illustration

3.4.2 Expected benefits for the client

In this chapter the client benefits of a law firm's website are analysed. The analysis is based on the functional areas as defined in chapter 3.4.1 and each possible client benefit is examined here, according to the functional area it is deriving from. The benefits model introduced in this chapter serves as the basis for the hypotheses in chapter 4 which are verified with empirical data in chapter 5.

First, the possible client benefits coming from the functional area 'access to law firm' will be analysed in detail.

- Access to law firm worldwide: The law firm's website allows for the clients to contact the law firm anytime and anywhere (e.g. via email) or find the nearest office including address and contact
- Access to detailed information on law firm: Apart from mere contact data, it is possible to provide the clients and prospective clients with a variety of extra information on the law firm, partners and associates. This is probably an interesting aspect for clients, as they can view a lawyers expertise (e.g. CV and experience description) or check on the law firms practice areas and the industries the firm usually works in.
- Access to global market information: The Internet gives all users the possibility to compare law firms, their expertise and their activities in the market place. Especially when contracting a new law firm this is probably of value to prospective clients.
- 'Put a face to the firm': The law firm's website gives the clients the possibility to view the partners and associates that are doing work for them instead of having a rather anonymous voice and name. Even partners and associates

that are not preparing legal advice for a client at the moment can add to the image the client has of the firm.

The possible benefits related to 'information providing' are:

- Access to basic legal information: Many websites contain articles published by the law firm or other publications on certain legal aspects. Although these publications are usually very basic they offer a good starting point for clients and prospective clients and allow them to gain a first understanding of a certain legal issue.
- Awareness of arising legal problems: Clients can become aware of arising legal problems through a law firm's website, e.g. by receiving a newsletter discussing a certain legal topic. This can help clients to avoid legal disputes and to prevent costly court actions.[70]

The functional area 'customised access' creates the following possible benefits for the client:

- Law firm is accessible from anywhere: The client can log into the law firm's extranet from (nearly) anywhere and can exchange files and data with the law firm or view the status of work in progress. Unlike a physical office the law firm's website is accessible around the clock. This makes the business relationship between client and firm less dependent on physical presence and office hours what is especially important for clients that travel a lot or live abroad.
- Only relevant information is displayed: Many clients have a busy workday and only limited time at their hands. Therefore a system that filters the information displayed to them and that makes suggestions for further reading or on interesting topics can reduce the work necessary to find the desired

[70] See SUSSKIND, R. (1998) page 45

information. This helps clients to get the needed information more easily.

The functional area 'online delivery' generates the following possible benefits:

- Access to detailed legal information and support: A law firm can offer detailed legal information, online support or access to certain databases to its registered clients. Although this service is not very likely to be free of charge, this could offer extra benefit to clients, as they would not have to search different sources for the desired information but they would have just a single access point that delivers all the information they need.[71]
- Service can be received anywhere: One of the outstanding features of the Internet in general is its ubiquity. This also applies for the websites of law firms and as the availability of the Internet is constantly increasing[72] it can be assumed that more and more clients will take advantage of it in the future. This means that the law firm's service is becoming less restricted by geographic boundaries.

The client benefits described in this chapter do not include such benefits as 'time saving' or 'convenience'[73] as clients probably expect these benefits from any website. Another reason why these benefits are not included is the fact that they rather result from the other benefits (as displayed in Figure 6) than that they are benefits of their own.

'Time saving' and 'convenience' are very likely perceived as general benefits by clients. The focus in this paper is on finding what could create these benefits, e.g. clients save time because they can

---

[71] See SUSSKIND, R. (1998) page xx, xxiv
[72] See SCHNELLER, J. (2004) page 8, 12, 32
[73] See and LOOS, C. (1998) page 37 and MEFFERT, H. and BRUHN, M. (2003) page 510

access detailed information on their contracted firm and their contacts easily on the firm's website.

Although benefits like 'time saving' and 'convenience' are not investigated in detail within this paper, they are addressed in the analysis of the interview results and the discussion of the hypotheses.

Figure 6: Possible client benefits of a law firm's website[74]

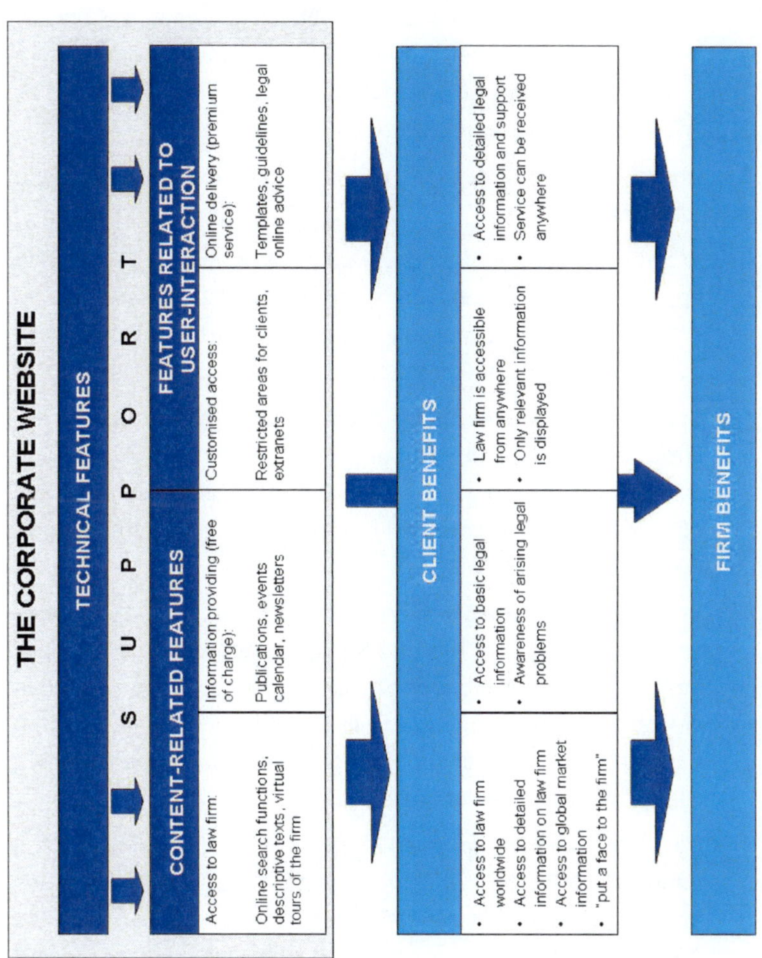

[74] own illustration

3.4.3 Expected benefits for the law firm

Considering previous studies on benefits of e-commerce and e-business there are several benefits that can be assumed to derive from a law firm's website. The possible benefits are examined here in detail according to the functional area they belong to.

The functional area 'access to law firm' creates these possible benefits for the firm:

- Appear to be available: The website enables the law firm to appear to be present 24/7 in the global market place. Although it is very unlikely that a law firm will always be available it can benefit from appearing available.
- Transport corporate culture / identity: The website gives the firm the possibility to introduce partners and associates and link its services to people and personalities. Just like any other information on the firm the website can help to transport the firm's values and identity to the clients.
- Improve brand / image: A corporate website is an opportunity for the firm to inform a broad audience about the firm's social activities such as pro bono work or sponsorships. This can create a positive image of the firm in the clients mind and the use of a corporate design and colour scheme helps the firm's clients to recognise the firm.[75]
- Better visibility in the market place: Being present on the Internet allows the law firm to be found via search engines around the world. If the website is linked to other websites and if it offers valuable content it can rank high on search engines and therefore it can be found by numerous clients.

The possible firm benefits related to the functional area 'information providing' are:

[75] See FRITZ, W. (2004) page 172 et seq.

- Demonstrate expertise and skills of lawyers: Publications on the law firm's website show the clients that the partners and associates are up-to-date on current legal developments and they can be an indicator for the skills and expertise of an individual lawyer.
- Show activities organised by law firm: A law firm's website is a good means of informing clients and prospective clients of activities organised or supported by the law firm. This could range from client discussion forums on legal aspects or the organisation of exhibitions to the sponsoring of art or sport events.
- Create awareness for certain legal problems: The law firm can create awareness for upcoming legal problems e.g. by sending newsletters or publishing articles. This will often generate new business for the law firm, as clients want to avoid legal disputes and require therefore legal advice.[76]

The possible firm benefits coming from the functional area 'customised access' are:

- Feedback into marketing systems (eCRM): The clients' activities on the law firm's website can be monitored and used to generate a more detailed picture of each client. This can help the firm to build and foster relationships with clients.[77]
- Offer services that match clients' needs: The law firm needs to deliver services that match the clients' needs in order to stay competitive in the legal market. Monitoring each clients' online behaviour can help the law firm to align their services better with the clients' needs.

[76] See SUSSKIND, R. (1998) page 45
[77] See MEFFERT, H. and BRUHN, M. (2003) page 504 and FRITZ, W. (2004) page 305 et seq.

- One-to-one marketing: Law firms are increasing their marketing spending each year[78] and being able to spend the budget on more effective marketing activities that reach the target group better can help to increase customer satisfaction and retention and can result in higher returns for the organisation.[79]

The functional area 'online delivery' generates the following benefits:

- Offer new services:[80] Modern information and communication technology helps organisations to offer new services to their customers, e.g. online delivery.
- Enter new markets:[81] It also helps the organisation to enter new markets, as it is possible for the organisation to reach customers that were out of reach before[82] e.g. clients that are looking for a law firm abroad and that don't have a contact in that country yet, can look the law firm and its expertise up on the Internet and make a first contact.
- Offer valuable legal content anywhere: The Internet allows the law firm to offer their legal services and advice globally without being personally present and not depending on office hours. Legal advice can be delivered by selling guidelines or detailed scripts online and modern communication technology allows for online delivery as well.

General benefits for the law firm such as 'cost reduction' and 'time saving'[83] that come from operating a website are not considered in this context. This paper concentrates on benefits from the firm-client-relationship with the main focus on the client benefits. Benefits for the

[78] See AUTHOR UNKNOWN (2004a) page 56
[79] See MEFFERT, H. and BRUHN, M. (2003) page 509
[80] See STRAUSS, R. and SCHODER, D. (2002) page 26
[81] See STRAUSS, R. and SCHODER, D. (2002) page 26
[82] See MEFFERT, H. and BRUHN, M. (2003) page 509

firm and possible other benefits that can be generated by providing a website would have to be examined in a different context.

Figure 7: Possible firm benefits of a law firm's website[84]

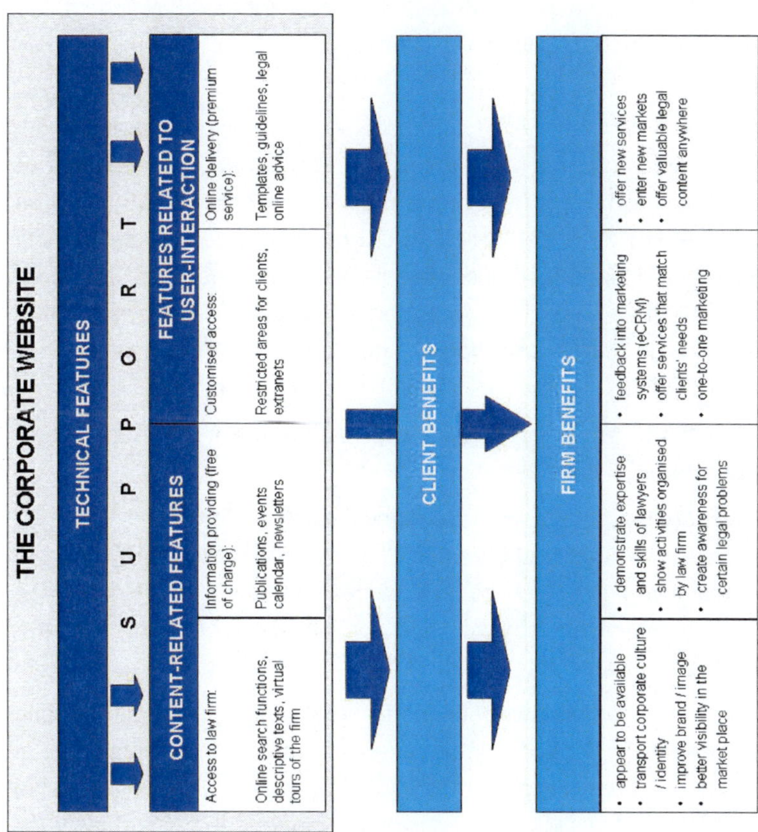

[83] See and Loos, C. (1998) page 37 and Meffert, H. and Bruhn, M. (2003) page 510
[84] own illustration

4 The hypotheses

The literary research conducted in chapter 3 and the client and firm benefits defined in chapter 3.4 are the basis for the building of the hypotheses. This chapter gives a short description of each hypothesis and its origin.

There is a vast number of corporate websites on the Internet and it only makes sense to maintain these websites when organisations or customers have a benefit from providing and accessing them. It can be assumed that law firms get benefits from providing a corporate website as it would not make sense economically for them otherwise. Based on chapter 3.4.2 there seem to be a variety of possible client benefits that probably differ in their importance for the client. Therefore hypothesis 1 can be phrased as:

H1: Clients are offered a variety of benefits from a law firm's website.

The possible benefits can be classified by assigning each benefit to one of the four functional areas of a law firm's website. The functional areas of a law firm's website are 'access to law firm', 'information providing', 'customised access' and 'online delivery' and they are described in detail in chapter 3.4.1

Each client has his own reasons for accessing a law firm's website and is looking for specific information. Depending on the type of information and service the client is expecting to find, it is very probable that benefits for him will be generated by different parts (functional areas) of the website.

Although there are various reasons for accessing a law firm's website, presumably some functional areas offer more benefit to more clients than others. Therefore it can be assumed that there is a hierarchy of the functional areas, depending on the benefits they offer. Hypothesis 2 can be formulated as:

H2: The four functional areas have different influences on the client benefits.

It is assumed that the more benefits a law firm's website can offer to its clients that the more impact the website can have on the business relationship with the client. In order to offer the most benefits to its clients the law firm has to align its online strategy with its clients' needs, without neglecting the corporate and business strategy though.

The better the firm has aligned its online strategy with the clients' needs, the more positive is the impact of the website on the relationship. A website that does not offer any (or hardly any) benefit to the clients has a negative impact on the relationship. Therefore hypothesis 3 can be stated as:

H3: A law firm's website has an impact on the business relationship between firm and client.

The hypotheses that are built in this chapter are verified or rejected through empirical research in the next chapter.

5 Empirical verification of the hypotheses

The hypotheses as defined in chapter 4 need to be validated through empirical evidence. This chapter explains the used methodology and the selection of the interviewees and summarises the results of the interviews. At the end of this chapter the results are viewed in the light of the used method and suggestions for further research are made.

5.1 Methodology

Previous studies examined customer preferences concerning e-commerce and website design but a publicly available study examining the customer benefits of a website whether real or perceived has not been conducted yet. As the client benefits of a law firm's website have not been examined either it is necessary to explore the expectations of clients and the degree of current fulfilment in order to recommend an online strategy for law firms.

The chosen interview method for this survey is the telephone interview. As there is no clear understanding of the clients' needs concerning the websites of law firms so far it seems to be the right approach. The telephone interviews allow for in-depth information as they are not limited by a strict structure but each interview can be adapted to the interviewees needs and additional questions can be asked to ensure that the given answers are understood correctly.[85] The set-up of the interviews is designed to gain valuable information about the experiences and expectations of clients concerning the websites of law firms which are then used to support or reject the hypotheses.

The interviewees are selected by company to reflect the client structure of a specific international law firm and by position within the company to ensure the relevance of their answers. During the interview

[85] See CZINKOTA, M. R. and KOTABE, M. (2001) page 131 et sqq.

the interviewees are asked several questions concerning the websites of law firms as well as questions regarding their demographic characteristics and general online behaviour.

The interview guideline[86] is tested and fine-tuned before the actual interviews take place. The results are analysed and interpreted and are then discussed in the context of the hypotheses. The recommendations for future online strategies of law firms are made, based on the findings of the survey.

5.2 Objectives

The aim of this survey is to gain a good understanding of the needs and expectations of clients and prospective clients concerning a law firm's online activities and how they can be improved in the future. The information obtained through the survey should be detailed enough to validate the hypotheses and give a first impression on the current situation in the legal sector. The results should allow for recommendations concerning future online strategies for law firms.

5.3 The interviewees

The interviewees are selected from the database that was compiled in 2002 by a student who wrote her thesis[87] for a specific international law firm. The sample structure reflects the client structure of that specific firm.

5.3.1 Detailed interviewee analysis

The interviewees are selected from a database that includes organisations from different branches, which have a legal department and therefore they probably work together with international law firms. It

---

[86] The complete interview guideline is attached in the appendix.

is very likely that not all organisations can or want to participate in the survey and in order to create significant groups the organisations in the database are classified in 4 categories rather than being grouped by industry type.

- **Companies under public law** – this category includes governmental and official institutions as well as organisations owned by the public.
- **Service & trade companies** – this category includes organisations that offer services or trade
- **Producing companies** – this category includes producing companies from a variety of industries.
- **Companies in the financial and insurance sector** – this category includes financial institutes and insurance companies.

The interviewees are selected from the 4 categories with the following ratio to reflect the client structure of a specific international law firm:

[87] STROHBAND, J. (2002) Diplomarbeit 'Einfluss von Rahmenbedingungen und Preisstrategien auf Kundenzufriedenheit und Kundenbindung' Universität Frankfurt am Main, Fachbereich Soziologie)

Figure 8: Interviewees per category

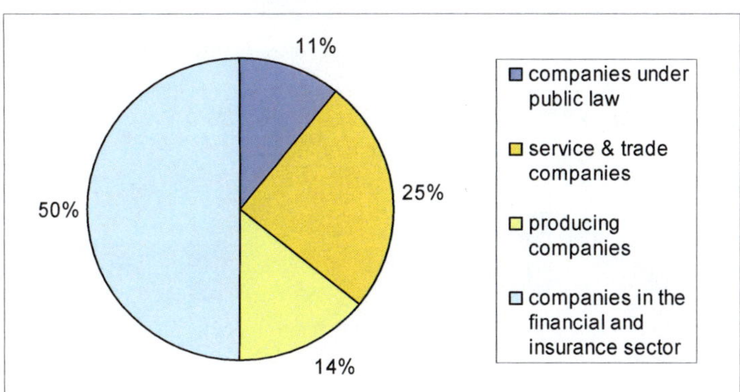

In total, 48 potential interviewees are contacted and 28 agree to take part in the survey. The main reasons for not participating in the interview are 'no use of the Internet at work' (6 organisations), 'no in-house legal department' (4 organisations) or 'no permission to take part in surveys' (6 organisations). The number of refusals adds up to 20. All results are presented in relative numbers although the sample size is rather small. The advantage of this is that the scales of the graphs can be compared more easily and the presented information can be assessed quicker.

All interviewees are working in the legal department of their organisation with nearly 70% of them being head of legal department or syndic. As these are usually the decision makers when it comes to contracting a law firm[88] their answers can be considered as significant. The position of the interviewees in the organisation is shown in detail in Figure 9.

[88] See AUTHOR UNKNOWN (2004f) page 21 and 58

Figure 9: Position in organisation - overview all categories

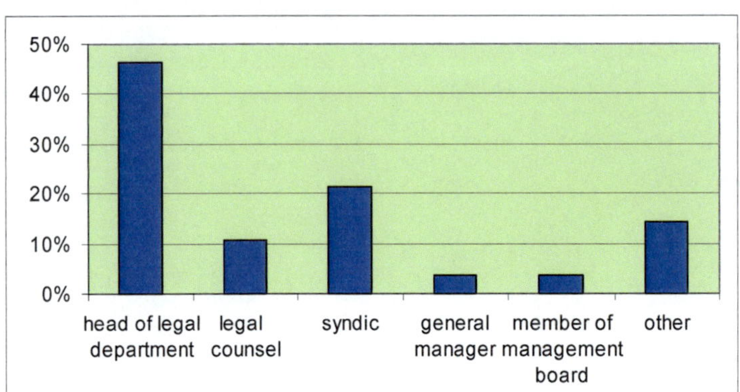

About three quarters of the interviewees are male, roughly 80% of them are lawyers and the majority (nearly 50%) of them are between 31-40 years old. This indicates that most interviewees are familiar with the legal market and considering other Internet studies the majority of them are probably experienced with Internet use. as the age group between 31-40 years is the demographic group with the most Internet users.[89]

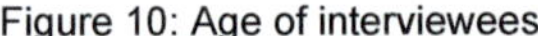

Figure 10: Age of interviewees

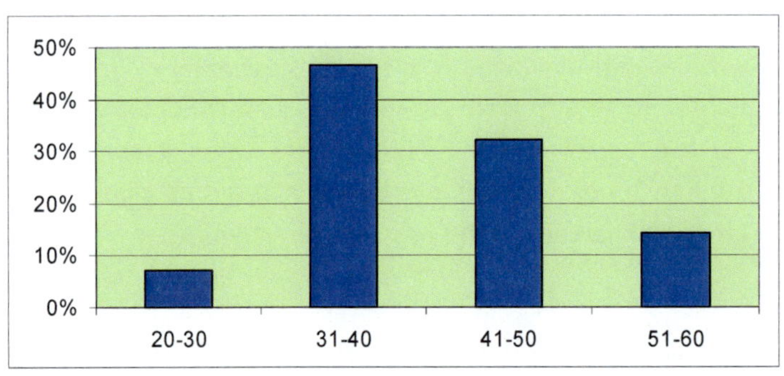

[89] See AGIREV (2003) page 12, 14 and W3B (2004)

More than a third of the interviewees spend 3-4 hours per week on the Internet and nearly 40% of them spend even 8 or more hours per week on the Internet. As can be seen from Figure 11, employees working in producing companies or in the financial and insurance sector tend to spend more time per week on the Internet than those working in service & trade companies and in companies under public law.

This indicates that the majority of the interviewees are comfortable with using the Internet and it can be assumed that especially those that use the Internet more than 8 hours a week are experienced users that have accessed a variety of different websites.

It has to be mentioned that Figure 11 only indicates the weekly Internet use in hours, as all interviewees can only give estimates of their time spent on the Internet. Therefore the scale on the abscissa has to be understood as an indicator of the hours spent and not as an exact measurement of time.

Figure 11: Weekly Internet use in hours per category

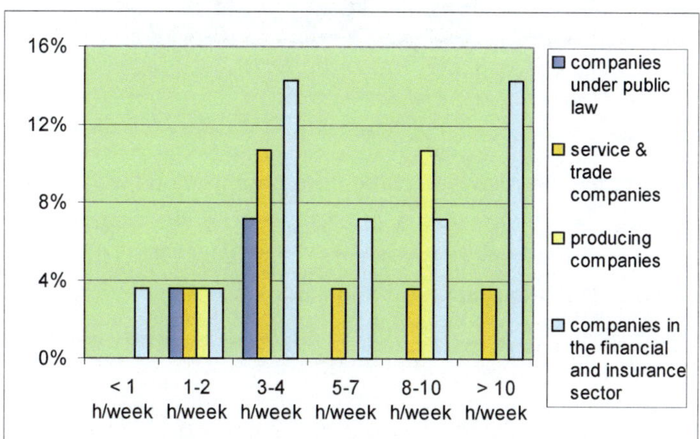

Most interviewees state that they use 4-5 law firms regularly at work and more than 90% of them have at least once a week contact with a law firm, with more than 60% of them working together with law firms everyday.

This implies that the interviewees know the legal market well and that they are clients of at least one law firm. As many of the interviewees require legal support for business and financial decisions it can be assumed that the majority of them are working together with internationally operating law firms.

Figure 12: Number of law firms used regularly - all categories

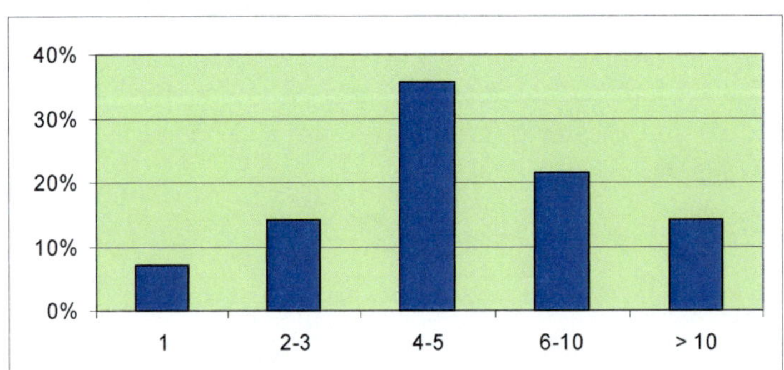

Nearly 70% of the interviewees come from organisations with more than 1.000 employees. As the focus of this paper is on clients and prospective clients of international law firms, it is very likely that the interviewees belong to this target group and it can be assumed that they would preferably contract big and international law firms if legal problems arise.

Figure 13: Number of employees - all categories

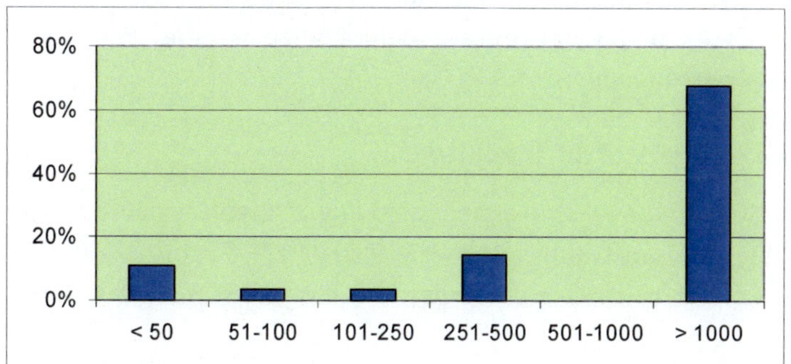

5.3.2 Summary of the interviewee analysis

Due to the sample size the survey cannot be a statistically valid survey but nevertheless the demographic data of the sample suggests, that the interviewees are clients and prospective clients of international law firms and that their answers represent the opinion of this group.

All interviewees work in the legal department of their organisation and they mostly are the decision makers. They all work together regularly with law firms, many of them even on a daily basis. Considering the types of law in which the interviewees usually require legal support indicates that they mostly work together with bigger and internationally operating law firms.

All interviewees use the Internet and the majority of them are frequent users. Therefore it can be assumed that they are familiar with Internet technology and the use of websites in general.

5.4 The Interviews

The initial phone call is made to inform the potential interviewee about the purpose and the structure of the interview and once he agreed to take part, a time and date for the interview is fixed. Each interview lasts between 20-30 minutes and the interviewees receive the summarised results of the survey as remuneration for the time they spent answering the questions.

5.4.1 Detailed analysis of the interviews

The results of the survey are presented in this chapter according to the order of the questions in the interview guideline.[90] Exactly as in the interviewee analysis all results are presented in relative numbers here as well.

5.4.1.1 How many websites of law firms have you accessed in the last 12 months?

The number of law firms' websites visited in the past seems to be dependent on the general Internet use of the interviewee, as those interviewees that use the Internet more frequently have also visited more websites of law firms. More than 50% of the interviewees have visited more than 5 websites of law firms in the past 12 months; some have even visited up to 40 websites of law firms. On the other hand there are nearly 18% that have not visited a single website of a law firm in the past. Reasons for not visiting are lack of time and one interviewee states, *"I have been working with the same contacts and the same law firms for years, and it just never crossed my mind to access their website."*

[90] The complete interview guideline can be viewed in the appendix.

Figure 14: Number of law firms' websites visited in the last 12 months per category

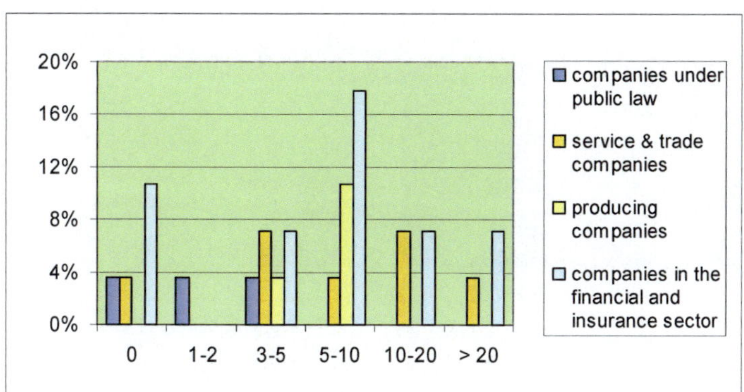

5.4.1.2 How often do you visit websites of law firms?

Many interviewees use law firms' websites regularly with nearly 50% using them at least once a month. Although none of the interviewees claims to visit websites of law firms on a daily basis several state that they visit one at least once a week.

Especially these interviewees who only work with few law firms and that do not use the Internet extensively state that they never or hardly ever visit the websites of law firms. While those interviewees who work with several law firms and who are frequent Internet users claim to visit law firms' websites more often.

It is noteworthy that interviewees working in the financial and insurance sector are those that visit the websites of law firms most frequently.

Figure 15: Frequency of visits to law firms' websites - all categories

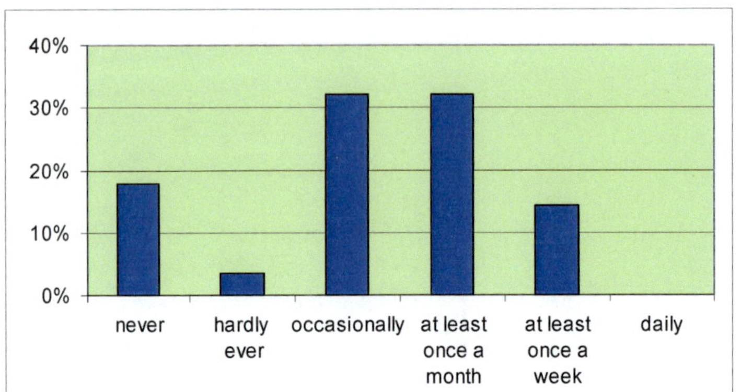

5.4.1.3Why did you visit the websites of these law firms?

The interviewees' online activities are concentrated on the websites of their appointed law firms but they also access websites of other law firms out of curiosity or because a special need arises.

As shown in Figure 16 there are various reasons for visiting a law firm's website but in general it can be said that nearly all interviewees look for contact details of the law firm and its partners and associates or for detailed information on the lawyers, including their practice areas and expertise.

Contact details (like phone numbers, email addresses and sometimes office addresses) are the most frequently named reason for accessing a law firm's website (~70%). Many interviewees state *"I could not find the telephone number of my contact and I looked it up on the law firm's website really fast."* Around 40% of the interviewees look for additional information on lawyers, such as pictures, CVs, proof of expertise, etc. because they have met somebody or heard or read about somebody and want to find out more. *"The keyword is 'business intelligence'. If a lawyer, that I don't know yet, is working for the opposing party I surely want to know more about him."* Information on the law firm's practice areas in general and information on the organisational structure are also very popular with nearly 36% of the interviewees stating it as a reason for visiting law firms' websites.

Reasons for not visiting a law firm's website or for only visiting it occasionally are mostly lack of time to browse and lack of a specific need to do so. One interviewee states, *"If I had the time to browse I would certainly have a look on the websites of the firms I am working with. But as I don't have a real need to do so, I just never get round to it."* This is supported by another interviewee who says, *"I only work with one law firm and if I need something I just give them a call."*

More than one reason could be stated and therefore the numbers do not add up to 100%. The reasons for visiting a law firm's website in the past give a good first impression of the interviewees' motivation for accessing law firms' websites. Considering the reasons for visiting a law firms' website it is obvious why the websites of law firms are usually not visited on a daily basis.

Figure 16: Reasons for visiting a law firm's website in the past

5.4.1.4What were your expectations before you accessed these websites?

The answers to this question can be grouped under the two main aspects – content and structure. All answers to this question showed that the interviewees' expectations are similar to the reasons for their past visits to a law firm's website. But they expect to find many more functions than they actually used in the past.

The analysis of this question also contains the statements of those interviewees that had not accessed a law firm's website until then. But as they had very clear perceptions of what they are expecting of a law firm's website, their answers are relevant too.

When asked to rate their expectations nearly all interviewees have problems to build a clear hierarchy of their expectations and to name those that are the most important to them. Single features and functions are important to them but the difference in importance seems to be marginal. As it is not possible to weigh the different expectations in this survey, they are only quantified in this paper, this means, if a certain expectation is stated it is assumed to be important.

The interviewees' expectations regarding the content of a law firm's website are rather simple. They expect to find contact details, detailed information on partners and associates and information on the firm's practise areas. *"If there is a new partner in a law firm I know I want to find out more about that person. I am interested in seeing his face and in finding some background information on him." "The lawyer is more important than the firm. Business is done by people not by companies. I only look for detailed information of partners and associates."* Only a minority of interviewees expect publications and information on legal decisions. The others do not expect this on a law firm's website as they do not think that it is the core business of a law firm.

Only one interviewee does not expect anything from a law firm's website and he states, *"I would expect to find all that bullshit that you usually receive as print material as well."*

Figure 17: Expectations concerning the content of a law firm's websites

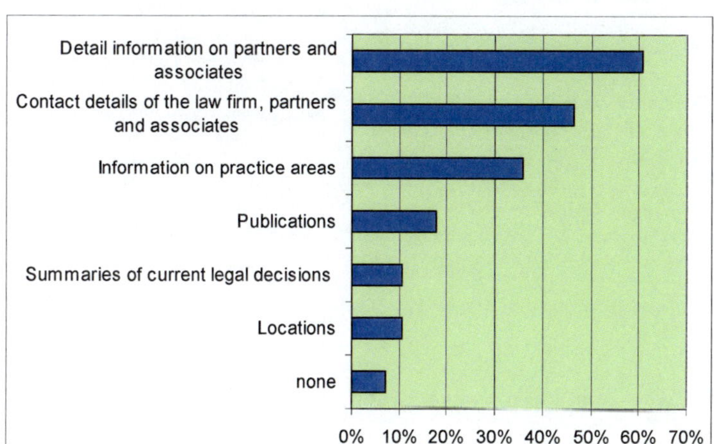

The expectations regarding the structure of a law firm's website seem to be similar to those of other websites. The interviewees expect the website to be clearly structured, concise and fast to access. All features that could distract from the content are not desirable in the eyes of the interviewees. *"The website should help me to access the information I want fast. Big graphics or flash-intros that take ages to load are very irritating."* Other expectations regarding the structure are, that the page *"[...] is formally correct and compliant with current law."* It should also not be to elaborate. *"It should be technically functioning and it should work on my computer without installing any other program."*

Figure 18: Expectations concerning the structure of a law firm's websites

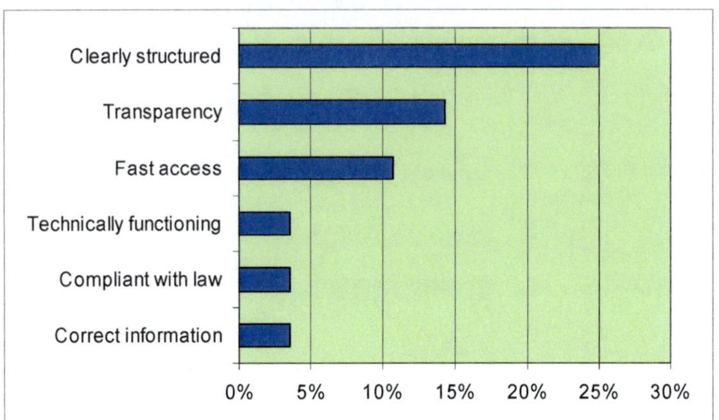

5.4.1.5Did the websites you accessed fulfil your expectations?

The interviewees' answers to this question show clearly that there is still a lot of room for improvement. The majority of interviewees are only partially satisfied with what they find on law firms' websites and often feel that the content is not presented to them in the right way.

But there seems to be a tendency that things are improving slowly and that several law firms are developing in the right direction. One interviewee states, *"Generally speaking, websites are improving when it comes to displaying the content, structure and clarity. And nowadays I find what I am looking for far more easily than I used to a couple of years ago"*

Those interviewees that were not or only partially satisfied had many different reasons for their dissatisfaction, but some answers were reoccurring. Interviewees state that some websites are very complex (and sometimes way too complex) with an incredible amount of information. *"Some websites are so complex that it is really hard to find the information you are looking for."* or *"Some websites are horrible and a simple phone book entry would be better for these firms."*

But some interviewees are satisfied with what they find on the websites of law firms they visit and they say, *"The last website I visited is nearly perfect!"* or *"I found everything I was looking for and the information on the website answered all my questions."*

Figure 19: Fulfilment of expectations

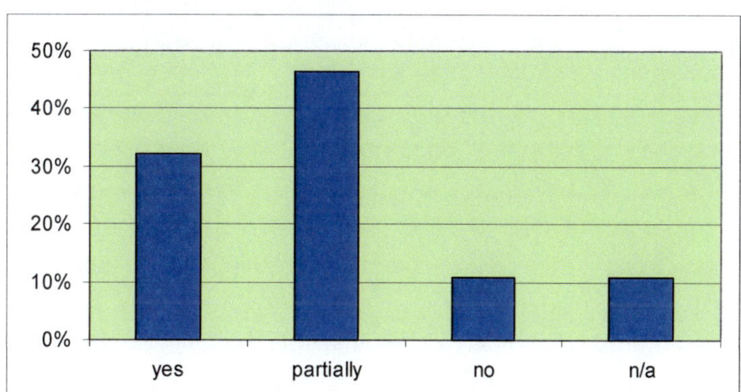

5.4.1.6What benefits did you get from visiting these websites?

The difference in importance of each benefit could not be measured, as the differences are perceived as only marginal by the interviewees. Therefore a stated benefit is regarded as important, while a not-stated benefit is regarded as rather unimportant. The interviewees could name more than one benefit and therefore the percentages do not add up to 100%.

The main benefit that most interviewees state to have received in the past is *"I find the desired information faster on the Internet than in books or directories. And I am online anyway."* Therefore their main benefit is that they can receive the desired information using their favourite means of information and of course the fact that they receive the information they are looking for. As most interviewees are looking for contact details and detailed information on the firm and its partners and associates it can be assumed that they receive a benefit from the accessibility of the law firm.

The benefits that rank second and third are 'time saving' and 'convenience'. They probably rank so high because they are rather general benefits that are associated with the Internet and, in particular, with law firms' websites. But especially the answers regarding 'time-saving' are contradicting. Some interviewees say *"The Internet is so much faster than any other source and often far more detailed and up-to-date."* while others think that *"It does not save time to visit the firm's website, but it is nice for a change and I can do it anytime I want without being put on hold.."* But overall 25% of the interviewees state that 'saving time' is a benefit they get from a law firm's website. Initially this type of benefit was excluded from the analysis but, as 'time saving' scored second and 'convenience' scored third on the list of perceived benefits, they have to be mentioned here in the analysis.

A benefit that several interviewees state is, *"I can satisfy my curiosity and look my opponent up on the Internet."* Another benefit for the interviewees seems to be the fact that they can search anonymously on the Internet. *"I like the fact that I can look for information anonymously. It would be awkward to call up the opposing law firm and ask for details on my opponent."*

Figure 20: Benefits of a law firm's website

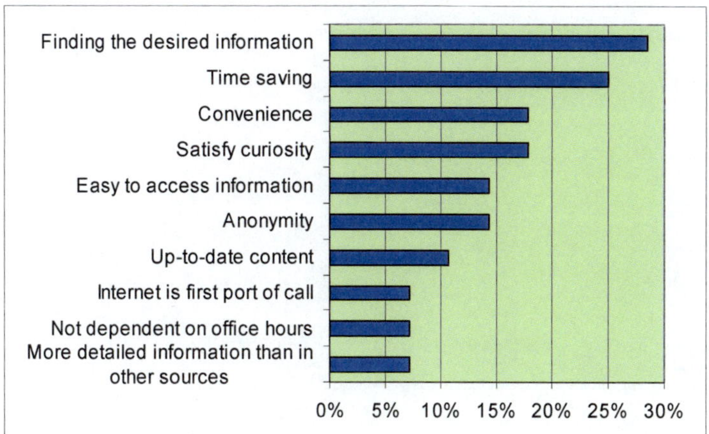

5.4.1.7 How often do you plan to visit websites of law firms in the future?

The interviewees' use of law firms' website seems to be rather continuous, as their predictions on their future use show a pattern similar to their past visits. But there is a tendency that the interviewees will use the websites a little less than they did in the past because *"The precise reason for past visits does not exist anymore."* Another interviewee states *"I'll visit a law firm's website only if I have a reason for doing so. But sometimes you end up on a law firm's website by coincidence, after searching a certain term on the Internet."*

The majority of interviewees expect their future online behaviour to stay the same because they expect that the reasons for their visits to law firms' websites stay the same. *"I'll visit these websites several times a month, just like I did in the past. That way I am up-to-date with current changes."*

Interviewees that visited law firms' websites never or hardly ever in the past, currently do not see a reason for changing their habits and one interviewee states *"If I would expect to benefit from a visit to a law firm's website I would go there. At the moment I can't really see that happening though."*

Figure 21: Probability of future visits to law firms' websites

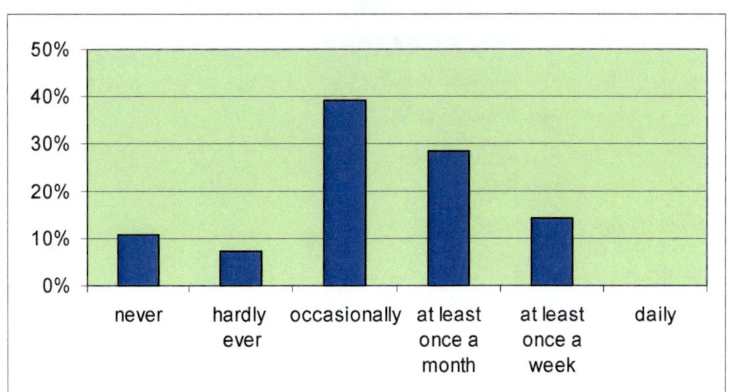

5.4.1.8Which other services would you like to find on law firms' websites in the future?

Clients and prospective clients are not a homogenous group and therefore their personal preferences and their business needs differ. This can be seen clearly when looking at the answers to this question.

Many interviewees state that although they use the Internet frequently for a variety of purposes, there are limitations to its use. Some say, *"I don't think that the Internet is the correct way of finding or communicating with a law firm. I prefer to talk to them personally."* Others use law firms' websites already quite regularly for looking up contact details or searching for information.

Although the interviewees have very different perceptions of the usefulness of law firms' websites they agree on some general statements.

All agree that features like chat / deal rooms, which are quite popular in other industries, are of no use to the legal sector due to security and liability issues and the complexity of problems.

Another problematic function on a law firm's website is the providing of restricted areas for clients. The interviewees state, that although a restricted area has several possible benefits, they can not imagine using it for any legal transaction as they perceive it to be an insecure way of exchanging information. And even those interviewees that would consider using a restricted area for clients on their appointed law firm think that *"A restricted area for clients does not make sense for me at the moment as we are currently technically not that advanced that we would benefit from it and then we would have to remember just another set of passwords."* Others though, think *"The use of a restricted area would make our communication with the firm faster and less dependent on office hours."*

The interviewees' opinions on publications on law firms' websites differ from *"Publications are a good way of judging a lawyers expertise in a certain practice area."* to *"Publications on a law firm's website are usually rather basic and aimed at non-lawyers."* Many interviewees see the writing and publishing of articles not as the core business of a law firm and are therefore rather suspicious whether they could benefit from the information provided. Some think that publications are just another marketing means for the firm and that the firm wants to show their expertise on a certain legal field without offering a solution or useful information. Most interviewees would not explicitly look for publications on a law firm's website, but they search for certain legal topics with search engines on the Internet, which means they read publications on law firms' websites rather accidentally.

Many interviewees do not have any expectations regarding new services that they would like to find but they would rather see current services improved. Apparently some law firms do not even manage to display the basics correctly, one interviewee states for example *"It would be nice if I could look all contacts up on the Internet so far I can often just search for partners on a law firm's website, but the associate is far more often my direct contact."* Another interviewee says, *"It would be nice not only to find the contacts but also to be able to view all lawyers and associates working in a practice area and to see the connection and dependencies between them."* This clearly shows the interest of the interviewees in the law firm and its lawyers. Improving the contact data on the law firm's website can probably create additional benefit for clients.

Information several interviewees would like to find on a law firm's website in the future are fees and pricing agreements although this is a rather difficult topic for the law firms. A multitude of different pricing agreements exist and they are often subject to lengthy negotiations, therefore it would be very difficult for a firm to list their agreements and fees on the Internet.

There are a variety of challenges law firms have to face in the future. And although some interviewees do not want to communicate with their law firm over the Internet even those see the Internet as a good way for finding the correct phone number or email address and other detailed information of a contact. These interviewees feel that *"the website of a law firm is only another marketing tool."* but still they can benefit from a law firm's website. But others think that there will be future developments that make law firms' websites even more interesting. These interviewees are interested in using the Internet and other online services to enhance their relationship with the law firm, e.g. by sharing research databases, building extranets, etc.

5.4.1.9Do you think that a law firm's website has an impact on your business relationship with this law firm?

The interviewees' answers indicate that a law firm's website does not have a great impact on the relationship between the firm and the client. It has to be distinguished between an already existing contact and cases where no previous contact exists.

In case that a contact between firm and client already exists, the website of the law firm has a lesser impact than when no previous contact between the firm and the prospect exists.

An existing relationship can not be harmed easily by a badly designed or malfunctioning website as interviewees state *"I don't care how terrible the website of a law firm is - if they do a great job I won't complain about that."* Others agree that a bad website would not affect their relationship with the firm but one says, *"If the law firm I contracted has problems with their website and I can't access all the information I want, then I would complain about it."*

If there has not been a previous contact between the firm and the prospect the website could have an impact on the future business relationship. Nearly a third of the interviewees state that if it is their first contact with the law firm the website would influence them. One interviewee says, *"If it is my first contact with that law firm and the website is very poor than that would give me something to think about."* It is interesting that this is the opinion of other interviewees too. They feel that a poor website would have a greater impact on their future relationship with that specific firm than a well working website. But still this impact would be rather marginal as the website is not regarded as a good basis for judging the expertise and capabilities of the law firm and its lawyers. But the website helps to create a general picture of the law firm and as it is a reflection of the firm on the Internet it can have an impact on new business contacts.

The majority of the interviewees feel that a website would not have an impact on their relationship with the firm, no matter whether the relationship already exists or not. One interviewee states, "*Contracting a law firm has to do with experience and not with the presentation on the*

Internet." And some feel that *"With enough money everybody can have a perfect website."*

The number of interviewees that is at least influenced slightly by the website of a law firm is substantial and should not be ignored. It is likely that some of the other interviewees are also influenced by the website although they do not consciously feel influenced. If a client for example can not find the telephone number of his contact due to a badly designed website or frequent page breakdowns this could be very annoying and could lead to a rather negative mood when he finally talks to his contact. So indirectly this could influence the business relation between firm and client.

Figure 22: Influence of law firms' websites on business relation

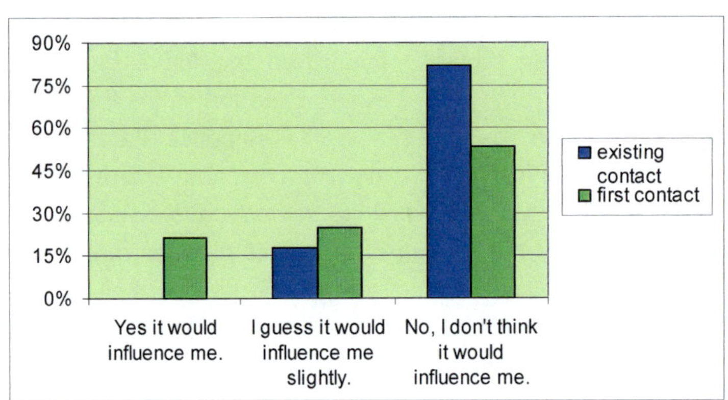

5.4.2 Summary of the interview results

The results of the interviews showed that the usage of law firms' websites by clients and prospective clients differs a lot. Some of the interviewees have visited more than 40 websites of law firms in the past 12 months, while others have not accessed a single website of a law firm so far. The majority of the interviewees have visited around 5 websites of law firms in the past and have therefore some experience with these websites.

Most interviewees state that they visit a law firm's website at least once a month, which does not seem to be very often considering that 60% of the interviewees have contact with law firms on a daily basis. But the interviewees' reasons for past visits give a good explanation for the rather little usage of law firms' websites. The reasons that were stated most often are the search for contact details and the search for detailed information on the firm and contacts. This is probably information that is not needed everyday and therefore the frequency of the past visits can be explained.

The interviewees' expectations concerning the content of a law firm's website match more or less their reasons for visiting such a website in the past and the expectations considering the structure of a law firm's website are probably just the same that anybody would expect from any website. They expect the website basically to be clearly structured and transparent. Nearly 50% of the interviewees state that their expectations are only partially fulfilled and only 30% state that they are satisfied with the websites of law firms they have accessed. But the general opinion seems to be that the situation is improving and that more and more firms are offering satisfying information on their websites.

The main benefit for the interviewees is to find the desired information, in this case mainly contact details and detailed information on the law firm and its partners and associates. Apart from that, many interviewees state that they like to look up information on law firms' websites as it saves time, satisfies their curiosity and they can conduct their research anonymously.

The frequency of future visits to law firms' websites seems to stay more or less the same and many interviewees state that they do not expect to access such websites more often in the future as they do not see a reason for that.

The expectations regarding possible future services on law firms' websites differ but most interviewees agree that if the already existing services could be improved they would be more satisfied with the website in general. Additional services could be more publications and improved ways of contacting the law firm and finding the correct contact easier.

Although there seem to be situations when a law firm's website can have an impact on the business relation, this will only be a marginal impact. The majority of the interviewees regard a law firm's website as one way of contacting the firm and finding basic information on it. But when it comes to contracting a law firm they value personal recommendations higher than information found on the Internet.

5.5 Critical evaluation of methodology and suggestions for future research

The chosen interview method is the appropriate way of retrieving the needed information. The telephone interviews allow for a thorough understanding of the expectations and experiences of clients and prospective clients of law firms as this method facilitates the interaction with the interviewees and it ensures that the questions and answers are understood correctly.

The sample size is small, with only 28 interviewees and some of the results are, therefore, not significant and can only be used as indicators for future developments. But, as most interviewees are decision makers, it can be assumed that their perceptions of law firms and their attitude towards them has an influence on the decision making and the buying decisions of the companies. Therefore, it can be expected that a survey with a bigger sample size would lead to similar results.

The interview guideline was tested before starting the interviews with the selected interviewees. It contains a number of open questions and this helps to gain a deeper insight in the personal opinion of the interviewees and they can state their expectations and ideas concerning the websites of law firms without being restricted to given answers.

Most interviewees gave explicit answers and provided additional information that adds extra value to the survey.

There are various limitations to the research though and future research on this topic could be conducted in order to verify the results of this survey and to gain further information.

Some suggestions for future research are:

- The survey could be repeated with a bigger sample in order to prove the results of this survey and gain more significant results.
- More in-depth information could be gathered by conducting one-on-one interviews with decision makers in companies from all industries.
- Another good means for gathering more detailed information on these issues are focus groups with the decision makers of the organisations. It would make sense to monitor a group of clients and prospective clients while they access websites of law firms. The way they use these websites and the problems they encounter could be used to further improve law firms' websites.
- It could also be very interesting to investigate which benefits can be generated by a law firm's website for the other user groups. Therefore it could be of interest to a law firm to conduct a similar survey with interviewees from the other user groups as well.

6 Applicability testing

In this chapter the findings of the survey will be matched against the hypotheses and compared to the current situation in the European legal market with focus on international law firms.

6.1 Discussion of the hypotheses

Based on the insights gained from the interviews, the hypotheses are discussed in this chapter. It will be examined if the hypotheses can be supported by the results of the interviews or not.

6.1.1 Discussion of hypothesis 1

The results of the interviews are used to evaluate the client benefits that can derive from a law firm's website and hypothesis 1 is validated.

H1: Clients are offered a variety of benefits from a law firm's website.

Each benefit as defined in chapter 3.4.2 is examined separately here and the found evidence is explained in detail. The evidence from the interviews is gathered and the possible benefits are evaluated. Due to the problem that the interviewees cannot assess the importance of single expectations or benefits because the perceived difference is too small, the evidence for each benefit is assessed here on a quantitative basis. The more interviewees state a single benefit the more evidence for it can be given and the more important this benefit seems to be.

- Access to law firm worldwide: Clear evidence can be found that supports the existence of the possible benefit 'access to law firm worldwide'. Interviewees state that *"The Internet is my first port of call as it is available everywhere."* and that *"It is so much faster to find contact information on the Internet than in books."* Altogether the information aspect was the number one reason for past visits to a law firm's website and it ranked second on the list of things expected on a law firm's website.

- Access to detailed information on law firm: Clear evidence supports the assumption that clients can get benefits from having access to detailed information on the law firm on the Internet. Several interviewees state, *"I find more information on the person that I am looking for on the Internet than in books and often it is more up-to-date than any print material."* This is reflected by the fact that 'detailed information on partners and associates' ranks second as a reason for a past visit and even ranks first on the list of expectations.
- Access to global market information: Some evidence can be found that having access to global market information offers benefits to clients. Although the interviewees agree that the influence of the information found on the Internet is only marginal as they rely heavily on recommendations, they state that they look up law firms regularly on the Internet in order to gather 'business intelligence'. One interviewee even states *"I was looking for a law firm in the United Arab Emirates, and as I didn't know anybody there I selected several firms over the Internet and made my decision after an initial contact."*
- 'Put a face to the firm': Clear evidence can be found that the interviewees expect to find photographs and other detailed information on their contact which helps them to create a clear picture of their contact in their mind. Many interviewees state that they have read or heard about somebody and later researched that lawyer on the Internet in order to be able to assess that person better.

- Access to basic legal information: Only little evidence can be found that supports the assumption that clients expect to get benefits from basic legal information that can be found on a law firm's website. Most interviewees agree that *"Publications on a law firm's website are just marketing material and they don't offer me a solution or useful information."* The general perception is, that these articles and publications are rather aimed at students and other non-lawyers. But most interviewees agree that, *"Publications are a good way of judging a lawyers expertise."*
- Awareness of arising legal problems: There is only little evidence that a law firm's website makes clients aware of arising legal problems. Most interviewees expect the law firm they are working with to point arising legal problems out to them. But few of them state that reading a publication on a certain legal problem could help them to assess their need for legal advice better.
- Law firm is accessible from anywhere: There is no evidence that clients perceive it as a benefit that they can access the law firm from anywhere. None of the interviewees states that he uses 'customised access' to a law firm's website although one interviewee states, that *"The law firm we are working with frequently updates information on our Intranet."* But the online services provided by many law firms are not used by a single interviewee.
- Only relevant information is displayed: There is no evidence that clients perceive a 'personalised' website that only displays selected information to them as beneficial. Interviewees state that in general they access the websites of the same law firms, usually of those firms they are working with and they state *"I know my way round the websites of the*

firms I am working with and I rather look around a bit, than remember another password."

- Access to detailed legal information and support: There is hardly any evidence that clients benefit from obtaining legal information and support online. Most interviewees state that they would rather pay money to get advice from a real person than pay money to receive some kind of legal document that is supposed to help them with their problem. They do not think that this would save them any time or hassle. But one interviewee stated, *"If the information provided on the website helps me to solve my problem without having to consult a lawyer, I would be willing to pay money for that."*
- Service can be received anywhere: There is only little evidence that the ubiquity of the online service offers benefits to clients. The fact that emailing and data-transfer systems make it much easier to receive documents and legal material is a benefit for clients, but generally the interviewees feel that this is not the right way of dealing with classified material, due to possible security breaches. But in some cases the interviewees appreciate the fact that they can receive the answer to a complex problem or a first statement from their lawyer online and everywhere. One interviewee states, *"If I am on a business trip and in a different time zone it is sometimes very convenient to be able to email documents or information instead of staying up late in order to reach somebody on the phone."*

As can be seen from the discussion above there is evidence for most of the possible benefits as described in chapter 3.4.2. Some benefits are supported strongly by the results of the interviews, for others there is only little evidence. The evidence from the interview results does not support all possible benefits, but there is clear evidence that supports hypothesis 1.

It has to be mentioned here, that there is also evidence for some of the benefits that are excluded from the benefits model in chapter 3.4.2. Especially 'time saving' and 'convenience' are very important to the interviewees and they rank second and third respectively on the list of benefits received from a law firm's website. The reason for this is probably that many interviewees are not aware of the factors that generate 'time saving' and 'convenience' but they are just aware of the perceived benefit. But the analysis above has focused on the underlying reasons for these benefits.

6.1.2 Discussion of hypothesis 2

The evidence gathered in the discussion of hypotheses 1 is used as a starting point for the analysis of hypothesis 2. The possible client benefits can be categorised in four functional areas ('access to law firm', 'information providing', 'customised access' and 'online delivery'), as described in detail in chapter 3.4.1. The spread of them over the functional areas has to be looked at closer, in order to support or reject hypotheses 2.

Hypothesis 2: The four functional areas have different influences on the client benefits.

In order to evaluate the influence of each functional area on the client benefits, they have to be ranked according to the degree to which they fulfil the benefits that are supposed to be delivered by them. In order to do so, the evidence gathered in the interviews, which has been used to validate hypothesis 1 will be used to validate hypothesis 2 as well. Each possible benefit can be assigned to a functional area and the evidence found for the benefits can be added up for each functional area. In order to so, the found evidence is translated into a points system, with clear evidence = 4 points, some evidence = 3 points, little evidence = 2 points, hardly any evidence = 1 point and no evidence = 0 points.

As each functional area offers a different number of possible benefits, the added points of each functional area are then divided by the number of total benefits in that respective functional area. This allows for a comparison of the different functional areas.

Figure 23: Influence of functional areas on client benefits

'Access to Law Firm'		
Possible Benefit	**Evidence**	**Assigned points**
Access to law firm worldwide	Clear evidence	4
Access to detailed information on law firm	Clear evidence	4
Access to global market information	Some evidence	3
'Put a face to the firm'	Clear evidence	4
		= 11
		11 : 4 = **3 ¾**

'Information Providing'		
Possible Benefit	**Evidence**	**Assigned points**
Access to basic legal information	Little evidence	2
Awareness of arising legal problems	Little evidence	2
		= 4
		4 : 2 = **2**

'Customised Access'		
Possible Benefit	**Evidence**	**Assigned points**
Law firm is accessible from anywhere	Hardly any evidence	0
Only relevant information is displayed	No evidence	0
		= 0
		0 : 2 = **0**

'Online Delivery'		
Possible Benefit	**Evidence**	**Assigned points**
Access to detailed legal information and support	Hardly any evidence	1
Service can be received anywhere	Little evidence	2
		= 3
		3 : 2 = **1 ½**

Using the described methodology the functional areas can be ranked. The functional area 'access to law firm' scores highest with 3 ¾ points and is followed by 'information providing' on a distant second place with 2 points. Rank 3 and 4 are 'online delivery' and 'customised access' with 1½ points and 0 points respectively. This ranking is of course just an indicator, especially as the sample size of the survey was so small, but it can be assumed that a larger sample size would have similar results.

Therefore it can be stated that there is clear evidence that supports hypothesis 2.

6.1.3 Discussion of hypothesis 3

It has to be examined whether hypothesis 3 can be supported by the interview results or whether it has to be rejected. During the interview the interviewees were explicitly questioned whether they think that the law firm's website has any impact on their relationship with the firm.

Examining only the answers to this question is not enough though, as it is possible that the website influences the relationship between the firm and the client, without the client actively noticing it. Therefore all relevant answers are used to find evidence for the impact of a law firm's website on the business relationship between firm and client.

Hypothesis 3: A law firm's website has an impact on the business relationship between firm and client.

Just like in the results analysis for question 9, a differentiation between an already existing business relationship and a new contact is made here, too.

If a business relationship between firm and client already exists, there seem to be other factors that have a deeper impact on the relationship than the firm's website. Many interviewees state that the personal contact with the firm is far more important to them than any technical supporting service, like the website for example. Only around 15% of all interviewees state that a law firm's website would have a minor impact on their business relation with that firm.

The probability that the website has an impact on the relationship increases, if other factors already made the client reconsider the relationship. One interviewee states, *"If I am already unhappy with the firm and thinking about a provider change, it would definitely influence me if on top of that the firm's website is of poor quality because it shows that they don't care!"* It is interesting to notice that the negative impact of a website seems to be bigger than its positive impact. A firm with a good website but whose service is rather doubtful can very possibly not benefit from the good website, but a firm with a poor website and a rather doubtful service can certainly be harmed by the quality of its website. This is supported by an interviewee who states, *"If I know the firm and their service is excellent their website can be absolutely trashy and I wouldn't care. But if I am not sure about the quality of their service and the website is horrible, it would give me second thoughts."*

If a business relation between the firm and the client has not been established yet, the situation is a little bit different. Several interviewees state that they think that the law firm's website would have a slight impact on their relationship, and nearly 20% even think that it would surely influence them and their perception of the firm. This means that the probability that a website has an impact on the business relationship more than doubles, if no previous contact has been made.

A possible reason for the impact of the website on the relationship between firm and client is of course the fact, that the website presents the firm to clients and prospective clients as well as to anybody else that visits the firm's website. The website is like a business card on the Internet and has therefore to reflect the firms image and identity. If the firm's reflection on the Internet is blurred or even obviously bad and misleading this has of course an effect on the clients' and prospective clients' perception of the firm.

On the other hand, if the website is designed well and has interesting content that offers value to the websites' visitors then it is a good opportunity for the firm to present itself and to show the expertise of its partners and associates in certain legal fields, e.g. through publications, proof of expertise, etc.

For both situations – existing contact and first contact – applies that the impact of the firm's website is rather marginal. But other factors (e.g. recommendation from colleagues, dissatisfaction with other parts of the firms' service, etc.) can influence the impact of the firm's website.

6.2 Current situation in the legal sector

The results of the interviews and the findings regarding the validity of the hypotheses have certain implications regarding the content and structure of a law firm's website. In this chapter it is examined whether law firms' websites are currently compliant with these implications.

This analysis is based on a study of the top 20 legal firm websites in the UK[91] commissioned by LEGAL IT[92] and carried out by INTENDANCE in 2004. The 'Top 20 websites' study evaluated each website with regard to content, design and usability. The findings of the study are assessed in order to see the compliance of the law firms' websites with the clients' expectations as ascertained in the interviews.

6.2.1 'Design' of law firms' websites

In the 'Top 20 websites' study high design scores were awarded for clarity of text, colour and balance between use of menus, text and images. Websites lost points if they were built using a frame structure because of search engine issues. They also lost points if they required the users to have software installed on their computers to view animations because of download issues.

The average score of design in the 'Top 20 websites' study was 82% but a closer look at the single scores shows that scores ranged from 96% (for Eversheds) to a mere 66% (for DLA). This indicates that while some law firms have already managed to design websites that are close to perfect, there are others that still have a long way to go before they can be considered as well-designed websites.

The results of the interviews suggest that design is not very important to the interviewees as long as it is not an obstacle to accessing the content. One interviewee states, *"I don't need many graphics and bright colours, just the plain content in an easy-to-read*

---

[91] See TUKE, J. (2004) page 14 et seq.

format - that's all I want." This is also supported by the fact that 'clearly structured' is the number one expectation regarding the structure of the website. When looking at the degree of satisfaction with law firms' websites it can be seen that while some pages seem to be consistent with the interviewees expectations or even better, the majority of these sites still fail to satisfy them.

According to TUKE[93] the website design could be improved by eliminating flash animations and implementing a frame-free[94] website structure. These changes require a rebuilding of the website though and are therefore resource consuming.

6.2.2 'Content' of law firms' websites

When it came to assessing the websites' content each website had to fulfil the minimum requirements of a legal website in order to take part in the 'Top 20 websites' study, e.g. information about the firm, the partners and their areas of practice. High scores were awarded to websites that had additional information e.g. up-to-date news, events and seminar pages, a publications section or links to other websites of interest. Firms were also given credit for providing multilingual information, and if their website enabled visually impaired visitors to access the content. Points were lost if the content was out of date or if information was missing.

In the 'Top 20 websites' study the average score for content was 82%, with the highest score being 91% (for Slaughter and May and Freshfields) and the lowest score being 73% (for Ashurst). But considering that several law firms have at least partly multilingual websites it is obvious that maintaining information updated is not an easy task.

---

[92] LEGAL IT is an online IT magazine for law firms in the UK and Europe
[93] See TUKE, J. (2004) page 14 et seq.
[94] A frame-free website structure will allow support-programs to access the page better, but it will make it more difficult to structure the page.

The results of the interviews show that the interviewees expect only a very limited range of content on a law firm's website; the most important information are contact details and detailed information on the firm and its partners and associates to be precise. Everything else, like publications and news feeds are perceived as 'nice to have' but not essential.

TUKE[95] suggests that some minor changes like including a downloadable firm brochure or posting current press releases and event information on the website would already improve the firm's Internet presence. This can only partially be supported by the interview results as these functions are not perceived as essential by the interviewees and they would benefit more from more detailed information on the firm and its partners and associates.

6.2.3 'Usability' of law firms' websites

The usability score was based on the ease of finding and extracting information. This included criteria such as the profile of the website on the search engine Google[96], the speed of file download, the navigation menus, the presence of a site map, etc. Websites lost points if they required the user to scroll extensively, if they did not provide 'printer-friendly' pages or if they did not have a site map in place.

Usability scored especially low, with an average score of 76%. The highest score was 88% (for Simmons & Simmons) and the weakest score was 64% (for DLA and Irwin Mitchell). This indicates that there is still plenty of room for improvement and that there are probably various improvement possibilities for law firms' websites.

There are no explicit statements on usability from the participants of the interviews, but there are certain requirements the interviewees state implicitly. Concerning the usability of a firm's website the

[95] See TUKE, J. (2004) page 14 et sqq.
[96] www.google.com

interviewees expect the website to be clearly structured and the information has to be easy-to-access. One interviewee states, *"Sometimes it just takes too long to find what I am looking for, then usually I give up and try another way of finding the needed information."* Many clients and prospective clients are short of time during their workdays and therefore they do not want to spend a lot of time searching for information. If the information can be extracted easily from the website the interviewees state that this satisfies them. One interviewee states, *"On the last website I visited I found everything I needed in a few minutes and it did not leave any questions open. This website was close to perfect."*

Most of the missing features that would increase the usability significantly only require minor changes in the website. Several firms for example did not have a sitemap on their website and many websites were not available in a printer-friendly format. According to TUKE[97] the use of dynamic menus and the minimisation of the need to scroll could increase usability as well, but these changes are harder to implement as they require significant changes in the websites structure.

6.2.4 Other important aspects

The 'Top 20 websites' study claims that it is expected of a law firm's website to have a client extranet facility and as most websites in the study had such a facility in place most of them did not loose points there. But the interviews showed no evidence that such a client extranet facility is of any importance to clients and prospective clients. This can be due to the small sample size, but it seems to be reasonable to question this expectation of TUKE[98].

TUKE also states that having online services such as micro-sites for careers and graduate recruitment are desirable for a law firm. No evidence for that can be found in the interview results, but as the target

[97] See TUKE, J. (2004) page 14 et seq.

group of the interviews is clients and prospective clients it is likely that this can be supported by a different survey design.

The 'Top 20 websites' study discovered that in general big law firms focus rather on the content of their website instead of making the information accessible and available for their clients. This may be caused by the *"extensive resources that a large law firm can rely upon to populate a website, while also highlighting the problem of how to organise and present such an extensive range of content without overwhelming the website user"*[99]. Although there is no explicit evidence for that in the interviews, it can be stated that several interviewees complain about websites that are difficult to access, which would support the statement that big law firms do not focus on accessibility and availability of the information on their websites. But interviewees also state that the information on the websites they accessed is not complete, e.g. no complete contact data, out-of-date information, etc. This does not contradict with TUKE's statement though as the results from the 'Top 20 websites' study revealed that none of the examined websites scored 100% for content.

Recommendations for future actions are made in chapter 7 based on the findings of the 'Top 20 websites' study and the interview results.

[98] See TUKE, J. (2004) page 14 et seq.
[99] See TUKE, J. (2004) page 14 et seq.

7 Recommendations for an online strategy

In this chapter the results of the survey are viewed in the context of common online strategies as explained in chapter 3.1 and online strategies for law firms are developed. Law firms have very different standards on their websites currently and are pursuing numerous strategies;[100] some of them focus on content and offer good information to their clients but have a rather complicated structure and navigation, while others have already improved their structure but still have content problems on their website.

After evaluating the online strategies in the light of the interview and research results, recommendations for possible online strategies in the legal sector are given.

7.1 Evaluation of common online strategies

INTENDANCE[101] claims that a law firm could aim at developing a 'brochure website', a 'marketing website' or a 'personalised website'. SUSSKIND[102] suggests that a law firm could aim at a 'brochure website', a 'legal library website', a 'legal discipline website' or a 'real life website'.

Considering the interview results there are certain types of websites that seem to be appropriate for a law firm while other approaches are not very suitable for the legal sector at the moment.

The 'brochure website' as described by INTENDANCE[103] and SUSSKIND[104] seems to be a good website type for the legal sector as the interview results show that clients and prospective clients expect to find information on the law firm and its partners and associates including

[100] see chapter 6.2
[101] See AUTHOR UNKOWN (2004e) page 17
[102] See SUSSKIND, R. (1998) page liv
[103] See AUTHOR UNKOWN (2004e) page 17
[104] See SUSSKIND, R. (1998) page liv

detailed information on all lawyers. Therefore providing a 'brochure website' would be the minimum requirement for a law firm.

The 'marketing website' as defined by INTENDANCE[105] seems to be an option for a law firm as well, although the task of creating and publishing content of direct interest to the target audience (e.g. articles on legal issues, guidelines, templates, etc) is a challenge for a law firm and requires relatively extensive resources. And the interview results show that publications and articles on a law firm's website are perceived as not useful by many interviewees, therefore the decision to invest in developing a 'marketing website' should be considered carefully.

A 'personalised website' as identified by INTENDANCE[106] can be an option for a law firm, but only under certain circumstances. The interview results show that many interviewees are not prepared to use a 'personalised website', either because they do not want to remember another password and also because some organisations do not have the technical requirements to use such a 'personalised website' effectively. But one interviewee states, *"We work together closely with our contracted law firm and they update information on our network regularly."* It is possible that 'personalised websites' become more widely used in the future. Currently many international law firms offer online services and extranets for their clients, and they are probably useful to them, but there is no evidence in the interview results that shows that firms should invest heavily in this area.

The 'legal library website' as proposed by SUSSKIND[107] might be possible in the future but currently it would be to resource consuming to be considered as a serious option by a law firm. Providing a multitude of books, articles and other publications with up-to-date content is a major challenge for law firms. At the moment several law firms are offering some publications and articles on their websites, but none of them can

[105] See AUTHOR UNKOWN (2004e) page 17
[106] See AUTHOR UNKOWN (2004e) page 17
[107] See SUSSKIND, R. (1998) page liv

be considered a legal library. And interview results imply that clients and prospective clients are not expecting to find extensive legal material on a law firm's website and many interviewees state that they do not expect to find useful publications at all on a law firm's website.

As a 'legal discipline website' is defined by SUSSKIND[108] as a further developed 'legal library website' the same arguments apply for it. Of course this could also be a future development but currently it is not applicable.

Therefore the fourth generation of legal websites, a 'real life website' as identified by SUSSKIND[109] is also not an option for a law firm at the moment.

7.2 Possible online strategies in the legal sector

It is not the scope of this thesis to define detailed online strategies for law firms, but the results of the research and the conducted interviews indicate that certain strategies are more likely to be applicable than others. The minimum functions and features a law firm has to provide on its website if it wants to create benefit for clients and prospective clients are described in the following. Then an advanced approach to offering benefits through a corporate website in the legal sector is outlined.

7.2.1 Minimum online strategy

The results of the survey suggest that there are certain minimum requirements for a law firm's website. If the website does not comply with these it is very likely that clients will not find it useful.

All interviewees state that they find it useful if a well working directory is in place on the website. This includes a search function by name and office for partners and associates. As this is the most

[108] See SUSSKIND, R. (1998) page liv
[109] See SUSSKIND, R. (1998) page liv

frequently used service on a law firm's website it makes sense to ensure that the information can be obtained as easy as possible and that it is updated continuously. Each lawyer should be presented in detail including his/her expertise, a short CV and of course the contact data.

One interviewee even states *"It would be nice not only to find the contacts but also to be able to view all lawyers and associates working in a practice area and to see the hierarchy in the department."* This is a very questionable suggestion though, as other problems might arise from displaying this information on the Internet. It is imaginable for example that clients would request to talk to a partner far more often than they usually do.

An online strategy of a law firm based on minimum efforts and expenditures should at least include the development and maintenance of a 'brochure website'[110] which gives a good overview over the firms' expertise and presents the law firm on the Internet. This enables clients and prospective clients to contact the law firm easily and to gather information on the law firm comfortably and therefore helps the firm to be visible in the market place.

7.2.2 Advanced online strategy

If a law firm is already operating a 'brochure website' it has to be decided whether the firm just wants to maintain the current status or if the firm wants to expand its online activities and develop a higher level website. This decision should not be made before all influencing factors are examined and it is recommended to survey the firm's clients (and other target groups) to explore their specific needs in detail.

Considering the online strategies as defined in chapter 3.1 the logical next step would be to develop a 'marketing website' and to add

[110] See AUTHOR UNKNOWN (2004e) page 17 and chapter 3.1

more functions to the firm's website. INTENDANCE[111] suggests that a law firm should include

- Information on seminars and events,
- Press releases
- Information on recent cases
- Publications and articles on legal issues
- Links to other useful sources on the Internet

The interview results support the providing of publications on a law firms' website if the publications offer a real benefit to the reader. For the other functions suggested by INTENDANCE there is no or hardly any evidence that clients are interested in them. But this can be due to the sample size and structure.

Apart from that the firm has to pay close attention to the basic information on the firm and ensure that the content is always up-to-date.

While expanding its online activities it is essential to monitor the websites' performance closely and to ensure that although it gains width and depth it still stays easy-to-use and informative. Especially the basic requirement (e.g. immediacy and accessibility) should not be neglected for the reasons explained in chapter 7.2.1.

It is also very important to ensure that no users are excluded from visiting the website due to technical problems and the use of animations and other multimedia elements. Anything that requires the user to download a program in order to view the content should be avoided. As some users might have a slow Internet connection the firm should pay attention that the file size is minimised in order to optimise download times.

[111] See AUTHOR UNKNOWN (2004e) page 17 et seq.

Some organisations in other industries design different versions (e.g. a HTML-version and a flash-version) for different user types and manage to avoid some of the technical difficulties with this.[112]

A more elaborate online strategy can be a way to differentiate from competitors as clients would turn to a law firm's website more often if it offers extra benefit. This extra traffic gives the law firm the opportunity to present itself to a greater audience.

7.2.3 Evaluation of recommended strategies

These recommendations are of course still very general and when developing an online strategy for a law firm further research should be conducted to ensure that all factors influencing that specific firm are known and that the expectations and needs of the respective clients are considered.

A considerable number of the organisations contacted for the survey do not use the Internet at work at all. Altogether more than 12% of these organisations denied taking part in the survey because of no or hardly any experience with the Internet in work life. The picture that these results show may of course be distorted due to the small sample size, but it is definitely something that should be considered when planning an online strategy for a law firm.

[112] See PIIRTO HEATH, R. (1997) page 54

8 Conclusion

The research conducted in this paper shows that the legal sector is very distinct from other professions, with distinct expectations regarding the use of law firms' websites. Although technically there are various possibilities for improving and enhancing the services a law firm can offer on its website, there are only a few options that currently seem to make sense to the company lawyers that took part in the empirical part of this study.

The empirical data indicates that there is no need for law firms to pursue a more elaborate online strategy at present as clients and prospective clients do not yet seem prepared to use such services as chat or deal rooms or integrated web and Intranet sites. And even the restricted areas that many law firms already have in place are not extensively used by clients and prospective clients. However, the interviewees acknowledge a certain potential for development and view it with a certain interest, but do not very much appreciate it.

The majority of the interviewees get benefits from functions related to the functional area 'access to law firm' which contains mainly all functions that allow a client or prospect to access information on the firm, to contact the firm and to gather market information.

Functions related to the functional areas 'information providing' and 'online delivery' which deal with legal content in various formats are not often used. This is noteworthy, as it would usually be assumed that legal content is received from a law firm directly. It seems however that the lawyers, who participated in this survey, do not generally use the websites of law firms for their research activities, although they often use other online sources for their research.

This is interesting behaviour that could be further examined by law firms in order to develop strategies to become more involved in the provision of legal information. The answer could lie in alerter services or partnerships with established providers for legal information. Currently clients and prospective clients use a law firm's website merely as an online directory or brochure and many possibilities are not explored and used.

It will be interesting to follow the developments that will take place in this industry in the next few years and to see if law firms and their clients and prospective clients will change their use of the Internet. There are certainly some client groups that are more likely to change their use of law firms' websites than others; e.g. the interview results showed that lawyers working in the financial and insurance sector use the Internet more frequently than their counterparts in other industries.

Experience from large law firms and their global banking clients is that virtual deal-rooms, electronic billing and online auctions, publications sharing and alerting of customised information are becoming more and more common practices and, are in fact, client requirements in the legal sector.

A change in the behaviour of clients and prospective clients will very likely also have an impact on the law firms. It will be interesting to see whether law firms react to this in the future and what developments this will trigger.

9 Bibliography

9.1 Books, Articles, Studies

- AUTHOR UNKNOWN (2001) CIM – Study Text – Advanced Certificate – Managing the Marketing / Customer Interface. Paper 5, London: BPP Publishing Limited
- AUTHOR UNKNOWN (2004a) Keeping score. In: The American Lawyer, 05/2004, page 53-59
- AUTHOR UNKNOWN (2004b) Im Schatten der Elefanten. In: JUVE Rechtsmarkt, 06/2004, page 10-15
- AUTHOR UNKNOWN (2004c) Hart am Wind – Kanzleiumsätze 2003: Weitere Konsolidierung in einem weiteren schwierigen Jahr. In: JUVE Rechtsmarkt, 10/2004, page 11-29
- AUTHOR UNKNOWN (2004d) The global 100. In: The American Lawyer, 11/2004, loose insert
- AUTHOR UNKNOWN (2004e) Solicitors' Websites 2004 – who is winning and why? London: Intendance Limited
- AUTHOR UNKNOWN (2004f) Seeing the world through clients' eyes - A study of FTSE-100 companies' perceptions of the UK legal profession. Twickenham: Nisus Consulting Limited
- AGIREV (2003) Online Reichweiten Monitor ORM 2003 II [online resource: www.agirev.de]
- CZINKOTA, M. R. and KOTABE, M. (2001) Marketing Management. 2nd edition, Cincinnati: South-Western College Publishing
- BETZ, J. and KRAFFT, M. (2002) Die Wirkung des E-Commerce auf die Kundenzufriedenheit und Kundenbindung. Koblenz: ZMU

- FASSNACHT, M. (1999) Relevanz der Kundenzufriedenheit für den Unternehmenserfolg. In: Herrmann, A., Jasny, R., Vetter, I. (ed.) Kundenorientierung von Banken. Frankfurt am Main: Frankfurter Allgemeine Zeitung GmbH, page 309-322
- FRITZ, W. (2004) Internet-Marketing und Electronic Commerce. Wiesbaden: Gabler
- HOEFLMAYER, D. (2003) Kanzleimarketing für die anwaltliche und steuerberatende Praxis. Berlin: Erich Schmidt Verlag
- HOSS, D. (2003) Die virtuelle Litfasssäule des Anwalts. In: Die Kanzlei, 01/2003, page 20 et sqq.
- HÜMMER, U. and JATZKOWSKI, A. (2004) Aufräumen in allen Bereichen – Blick zurück auf ein durchwachsenes Jahr 2003. In: JUVE Rechtsmarkt, 01/2004, page 21-26
- KENYON, H. (2000) E-business – succeeding in a dotcom environment. In: cover notes, 03/2000 [online resource: www.pwc.com]
- LOOS, C. (1998) Online Vertrieb von Konsumgütern. Wiesbaden: Gabler Verlag
- MADEJA, N. and SCHODER, D. (2003) Designed for Success – Empirical Evidence on Features of Corporate Web Pages [online resource: www.wim.uni-koeln.de]
- NEAL, C., QUESTER, P. and HAWKINS, D. (2002) Consumer Behaviour – Implications for Marketing Strategy. 3rd edition, Roseville: McGraw-Hill Australia Pty Limited
- NIELSEN, J. and NORMAN, D. A. (2000) Usability On The Web Isn't A Luxury. In: informationweek, 14/02/2000, [online-resource: www.informationweek.com]
- MAISTER, D. H. (1993) Managing the professional service firm. Paperback edition, New York: Free Press Paperbacks

- MEFFERT, H. and BÖING, C. (2000) Erfolgsfaktoren und Eintrittsvorraussetzungen im Business-to-Consumer-E-Commerce – ausgewählte Ergebnisse einer empirischen Analyse. Münster: Wissenschaftliche Gesellschaft für Marketing und Unternehmensführung e.V.
- MEFFERT, H. and BRUHN, M. (2003) Dienstleistungsmarketing. 4th edition, Wiesbaden: Gabler Verlag
- PIIRTO HEATH, R. (1997) Design a Killer Web Site. In: Marketing Tools, 05/1997, page 50-55
- RÖMERMANN, R. (2003) Anwaltliches Marketing Management – Der Weg zum optimalen Kanzleimarketing. Köln: Verlag Dr. Otto Schmidt
- SCHNELLER, J. (2004) ACTA 2004 - Entwicklung des Internet als Transaktionsmedium und im E-Commerce. Institut für Demoskopie Allensbach [online resource: www.ifd-allensbach.de]
- STEINBEIS, M. (2004) Bundesverfassungsgericht erleichtert Anwaltswerbung. In: Handelsblatt 13/08/2004 [online resource: www.handelsblatt.com]
- STRAUSS, R. and SCHODER, D. (2001) E-Reality 2000-Studie. Frankfurt am Main: FAZ Institut für Management-, Markt- und Medieninformationen
- SUSSKIND, R. (1998) The future of law – Facing the challenges of Information Technology. Paperback edition, New York: Oxford University Press
- TUKE, J. (2004) Best of the web. In: Legal week 26/08/2004, page 14
- W3B (2004) 19. WWW-Benutzer-Analyse. W3B. 11/2004 [online resource: www.w3b.de]

- ZEITHAML, V. A. and Bitner M. J. (2000) Services Marketing: Integrating customer focus across the firm. 2nd edition. Boston: The McGraw-Hill Companies Inc.

9.2 Homepages

- www.computerworld.com - Computerworld
- www.google.com - Google
- www.intendance.com - Intendance Limited
- www.legalit.net - Legal IT
- www.nisus.net - Nisus Consulting Limited.

10 Appendix

10.1 The interview guideline

Question 1: How many websites of law firms have you accessed in the last 12 months?
[0; 1-2; 3-5; 5-10; 10-20; >20]

Question 2: How often do you visit websites of law firms?
[never; hardly ever; occasionally; at least once a month; at least once a week; daily]

Question 3: Why did you visit the websites of these law firms?

Question 4: What were your expectations before you accessed these websites? What did you expect to find? How important is it for you to find what you expect?

Question 5: Did the websites you accessed fulfil your expectations?
[yes; partially; no]

Question 6: What benefits did you get from visiting these websites? How important are these benefits to you?

Question 7: How often do you plan to visit websites of law firms in the future?
[never; hardly ever; occasionally; at least once a month; at least once a week; daily]

Question 8: Which other services would you like to find on law firms' websites in the future? Which reasons for accessing such sites more often can you think off?

Question 9: Do you think that a law firm's website has an impact on your business relationship with this law firm?
[yes, it would influence my decision; I guess it would influence my decision; no, I don't think it would influence my decision]

Additional questions:

- How old are you?
[20-30; 31-40; 41-50; 51-60; >60]
- Gender?
[male, female]
- How many hours do you spend surfing the Internet per week?
[<1; 1-2; 3-4; 5-7; 8-10; >10]
- How often do you have contact with law firms?
[daily; at least once a week; at least once a month]
- With how many law firms do you work together on a regular basis?
[1; 2-3; 4-5; 6-10; >10]
- What is your position within the company?
[head of legal department; legal counsel; syndic; general manager; member of management board; other]
- Are you a lawyer?
[yes; no]
- How many employees does your organisation have at the moment?
[<50; 51-100; 101-250; 251-500; 501-1000; >1000]

Frankfurter Schriften zum Marketing für Finanzdienstleistungen

Herausgegeben von Prof. Dr. Ralf Jasny

ISSN 1861-0978

Das Thema Marketing für Finanzdienstleistungen ist für die Finandienstleistungsbranche eine vergleichsweise junge Disziplin. Erst in den 80er Jahren haben sich Banken und Versicherungen mit diesem Thema intensiver auseinandergesetzt. Anfänglich wurde versucht, die Konzepte und Vorgehensweisen aus der Konsumgüterindustrie zu kopieren, ohne dass dabei die Spezifika der Branche berücksichtigt wurden. Dementsprechend ist die praktische und wissenschaftliche Auseinandersetzung mit Marketing für Finanzdienstleistungen weniger ausgeprägt als in anderen Industrien.

Die Schriftenreihe *Frankfurter Schriften zum Marketing für Finanzdienstleistungen* setzt sich daher mit innovativen und praktisch hoch relevanten Fragestellungen zum Thema Marketing für FDL auseinander und beleuchtet ausgewählte Aspekte zum Thema Strategie, Branding, Pricing, Produkte und Vertrieb in allen Facetten. Damit schließt sie eine Lücke in der systematischen Auseinandersetzung mit Fragen des Finanzdienstleistungsmarketing und liefert damit wertvolle Diskussionsbeiträge sowohl für die Wissenschaft als auch für die unmittelbare praktische Anwendung.

Series Subscription

Please enter my subscription to the series *Frankfurter Schriften zum Marketing für Finanzdienstleistungen*, ISSN 1861-0978, as follows:

❒ complete series OR ❒ English-language titles
❒ German-language titles

starting with

❒ volume # 1

❒ volume # ___

❒ please also include the following volumes: #___, ___, ___, ___, ___, ___

❒ the next volume being published;

❒ please also include the following volumes: #___, ___, ___, ___, ___, ___

❒ 1 copy per volume OR ❒ ___ copies per volume

<u>Subscription within Germany:</u>

You will receive every volume at 1st publication at the regular bookseller's price – incl. s & h and VAT.

Payment:

❒ Please bill me for every volume.

❒ Lastschriftverfahren: Ich/wir ermächtige(n) Sie hiermit widerruflich, den Rechnungsbetrag je Band von meinem/unserem folgendem Konto einzuziehen.

Kontoinhaber: ______________________ Kreditinstitut: ______________________

Kontonummer: ______________________ Bankleitzahl: ______________________

<u>International Subscription:</u>

Payment (incl. s & h and VAT) in advance for

❒ 10 volumes/copies (€ 319.80) ❒ 20 volumes/copies (€ 599.80)

❒ 40 volumes/copies (€ 1,099.80)

Please send my books to:

NAME______________________ DEPARTMENT______________________

ADDRESS ____

POST/ZIP CODE______________________ COUNTRY ______________________

TELEPHONE ______________________ EMAIL______________________

date/signature____

Please fax to: **0511 / 262 2201 (+49 511 262 2201)**

or mail to: *ibidem*-Verlag, Julius-Leber-Weg 11, D-30457 Hannover,Germany

or send an e-mail: ibidem@ibidem-verlag.de

***ibidem*-Verlag**
Melchiorstr. 15
D-70439 Stuttgart
info@ibidem-verlag.de
www.ibidem-verlag.de
www.edition-noema.de
www.autorenbetreuung.de